CW00672870

SHIPWRECK
TO DORSET ANI
FOR DIVERS AND SKIPPERS

Written by Nigel Clarke

Local Editors: Nick Chipchase, Grahame Knott, John Walker, Jeff King,

Peter Williams, Ian Corwall, Ben Thomas, Douglas Lanfear, Simon Bassett and Nick Bright.

This book is dedicated to myself, as without me it would not have been published. All the mistakes are by some one else.

ISBN 0 907683 81 9

NIGEL J. CLARKE PUBLICATIONS

Unit 2, Russell House,
Lym Close, Lyme Regis,
Dorset. DT7 3DE
Tel: 01297 442513
Fax: 01297 442513

www.njcpublications.demon.co.uk
www.sw-marine-info.co.uk
email mail@njcpublications.demon.co.uk

Ten Most Modern Wrecks

Majorca 1982

Licence to Kill 1981

Saratoga 1981

Marie Des Isles 1980

Aeolian Sky 1979

Pergo 1975

Scaldis 1974

Greta.C 1974

Evertsen 1961

HMS Sidon 1957

The Ten Largest Wrecks

HMS Empess of India 15,585 dis

HMS Formidable 15,000 dis

HMS Hood 14,150 dis

Rotorua 11,130 gross

British Inventor 7,101 gross

Kyarra 6,953 gross

Binnindijk 6,873 gross

Pomella 6,766 gross

Aeolian Sky 6,540 gross

Miniota 6,422 gross

The Ten Oldest Wrecks

Haswell 1786

Earl of Abergavenny 1805

Heroine 1852

HMS Amazon 1866

Normandy 1870

Royal Adelaid 1872

Avalanche 1877

Alexandrova 1882

Brittania 1884

Nor 1887

Ten Sailing Vessels

Alexandrova 1882

Avalanche 1870

Earl of Abergavenny 1805

Halsewell 1786

License to Kill 1981

Lucinda 1914

Nor 1887

Perriton 1918

Royal Adelaide 1872

Siren 1896

Interesting Cargoes

Aeloian Sky- landrovers

Aeneas- sandals

Glenmore- diving equipment

Halswell- gold,silver

Iolanthe- railway trucks

Miniotta- silver bullion

Thames -tin ingots

FOREWORD

This is the second edition of this book, and I have attempted to take out some of the mistakes. Since the first edition about two years ago there have been numerous new wrecks found around the coast. Some of these discoveries will have to remain off limits to amateur divers due to the sensitive nature of the sites, and some are war graves. Towards the end of 2001, a new medieval wreck was found at Axmouth and the timbers have been dated as possibly fourteenth century. The site is visible at low tide, and while not spectacular, shows that one does not have to dive deep to find new wrecks.

I have expanded the book to cover the area to the east of Portland Bill, and included more wrecks in Devon. I still include the maps, which show the diveable wrecks in the area, but the number of wrecks included in this book now amount to over 203, which is an illustrator's nightmare to present in a chart. The wrecks shown are the most prominent and interesting. On the other wrecks I have included the position (if known) and background.

When I first started this project it seemed such a good idea and I never expected it to become so complex. When you examine the books on shipwrecks, you soon find errors in the information. The name, date or type of ship is not correct. No sooner is one error published and the same mistake is repeated in other journals, till the error seems then to become the accepted fact. It is only in the last few years that charting and naming of the wrecks has become more accurate. I have stated in the text if a diver has gone down and surveyed the wreck and positively identified the vessel. I have also attempted to remove as much of the misinformation from this book as possible, and always welcome feedback leading to a positive identification of a site.

There are numerous shipwreck sites on the sea bed of the Dorset and East Devon coast, many of which have fallen into decay or been broken by the action of storm, salvage or demolition. Diving is one area where the amateur can be of great assistance to the marine archaeologists by recording and reporting any finds. Many of the wrecks date from the First World War and contain unexploded ordnance items; these should not be disturbed - with the passage of time such items have become more unstable; many of the wrecks along this section of the coast are over seventy years old.

All wrecks host marine life; they provide a refuge on a bleak seabed, an oasis in a Spartan desert where life can flourish, but they also have the hidden danger of monofilament nets. Please beware of these nets when diving and always have knife.

Visibility along this section of the coast is always a problem; the clearest wrecks are around Portland, but there you have the problems of tide. The wrecks near Lyme Regis and West Bay can be marine fog-bound in the spring – caused by the algae growth that is known as "May Water". Storms can also reduced the visibility; if you are travelling a long way, check out the weather forecast and conditions with a local dive shop, who should be able to advise you.

The layout of this book -
Name of Vessel
Position (GPS)
Type of vessel
Tonnage - where known
Cargo - if known
Date of sinking: Year/ Day/ Month.

The vessels are listed in alphabetical order; to see the rough geographical position please look at the map, which is not to scale and only gives the approximate location of the wreck, and from this the nearest port. Some of the wrecks are more popular than others, and anglers fish many. To safely dive most of these wrecks, a knowledge of the tide times is necessary, and for many of the deeper wrecks I would recommend a local boat with knowledge of the area, although positions are shown it is often difficult to anchor on the wreck.

I have also spoken to some of the local skippers and divers asking them to name their favourite and most hated wrecks - see the following pages.

I would like to thank all who have helped me with this book; a full list is at the back, and I apologize if I have left anyone out.

HMS FORMIDABLE

4

RECOMMENDED BEST AND WORST LOCAL WRECKS

I sent out a questionnaire to a number of local experienced divers, and I asked them to name the wrecks in the following categories. You will note some wrecks appear in both the best wreck section and most disliked section. I have quoted the comments; in some cases it depends on the time of year you visit the wreck as to your opinion of the site. The divers responding to the questionnaire were all very experienced; here is their list of recommendations:

Name the most interesting wreck you dive on?

HMS M2 - Sank 1932 - Intact submarine off the West Dorset Coast. Recommended by two divers.

HMS BUCCANEER - Sank 1946 - Royal Naval tug, intact and interesting.

SALSETTE - Sank 1917 - Passenger Liner. Lyme Bay, west of Portland Bill.

St DUNSTAN - Sank 1917 - Bucket dredger. East of West Bay, Bridport.

KYARRA - Sank 1918 - Passenger liner converted to a hospital ship sank east of Swanage.

BAYGITANO - Sank 1918 - Steamer sank offshore from Lyme Regis.

HMS BODICEA - Sank 1944 - Destroyer sunk by the Luftwaffe.

BRETAGNE - Sank 1918 - Norwegian steamship schooner, sank off Exmouth.

LORD STEWART - Sank 1918 - Armed steamship, sank offshore between Exmouth and Torquay.

MODAVIA - Sank 1943 - Motor vessel, sank east of Torquay.

HMS LORD HAILSHAM - Sank 1943 - Anti-submarine trawler sank offshore east of Torquay.

CHATEAU YQUEM - Sank 1913 - Steamship, sank middle of Lyme Bay.

MOIDART - Sank 1918 - Steamship, sank south of Lyme Regis.

The ideal wreck for the new or novice diver?

COUNTESS OF ERNE - Sank 1936 – Portland Harbour

GALICIA - Sank 1917

HMS HOOD - Sank 1914 – Portland Harbour

BAYGITANO - Sank 1918

BETSY ANNA - Sank 1926

5

ROYAL ADELAIDE - Sank 1872 - Shore dive, Chesil Beach near Portland.

BRETAGNE - Sank 1918

The best intact deep-water wreck?

Some of these wrecks are in deep water, and the positions of two are only known to dive boat skippers.

SALSETTE

HMS EMPRESS OF INDIA

MINERVA

ISBJORN

POMERANIAN

MUREE - Intact tanker that sank in 1989, near the shipping lanes - good visibility. To dive contact Weymouth dive boats or any of the skippers listed at the back of this book.

ILLINOIS - Deep-water wreck. The Illinois is a container ship. Contact Weymouth deep diver charter vessels for a visit.

LORD STEWART

HMS AMAZON - A new wreck discovered in 2001. This wreck is of archaeological interest and only for visual inspection. Contact Weymouth Dive skipper Grahame Knott if you are interested in seeing this early screw powered warship, which is intact.

The most disliked wreck in the area?

The response was interesting; the submarine M2 was also one of top dive sites with other divers. It just depends if you sometimes have had a bad dive. This is a list of personal observations about these wrecks.

AEOLIAN SKY - "A tangled mess of metal, dark and dank".

POMERANIAN - "Blown apart silty with crap visibility" Ben of Portland Oceaneering.

MARGUERITE (BENNY'S WRECK) - "Heap of junk on the seabed"

GIBEL HAMAM - "Lots of nets on the wreck, tangled in the structure and poor viz." Les of Lyme Divers.

HMS M2 - "Too many dive boats with lots of divers during the peak of the season." Ian Cornwall of Lindy Lou.

GEFFIEN - "Broken up and not much to see" Jeff King of Exmouth Divers.

Recommended area for scenic dives for photographers and drift dives?

PULPIT ROCK Portland Bill

SAW TOOTH LEDGES of West Bay, Bridport, Dorset

EAST TENNENTS off shore from West Bay, Bridport, Dorset

WEST BAY HIGH GROUND West Bay, Bridport, Dorset

PEVERIL POINT deep drift dive. (Contact Paul Williams 07977 142661 Swanage based boat)

SWIRE LEDGES Chesil Beach

OTTER COVE East Devon

MERMAID ARCH East Devon

THE MUSSEL BEDS West Shambles off Portland

WEST BAY WALL. Shallow dive site. West Bay, Bridport, Dorset.

VISITING THESE LOCATIONS

If you are interested in visiting any of the sites above, there is a section at the back of the book which gives contacts for boats and skippers.

Diveable Wrecks in East Dorset

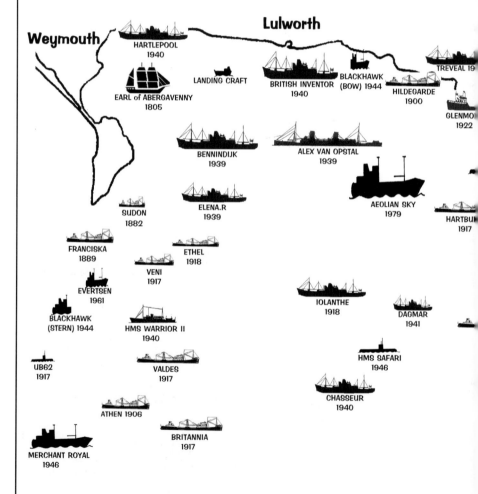

Weymouth

Lulworth

HARTLEPOOL 1940

EARL of ABERGAVENNY 1805

LANDING CRAFT

BRITISH INVENTOR 1940

BLACKHAWK (BOW) 1944

TREVEAL 19

HILDEGARDE 1900

GLENMO 1922

BENNINDIJK 1939

ALEX VAN OPSTAL 1939

AEOLIAN SKY 1979

HARTBU 1917

SUDON 1882

ELENA.R 1939

FRANCISKA 1889

ETHEL 1918

VENI 1917

EVERTSEN 1961

IOLANTHE 1918

DAGMAR 1941

BLACKHAWK (STERN) 1944

HMS WARRIOR II 1940

HMS SAFARI 1946

UB62 1917

VALDES 1917

CHASSEUR 1940

ATHEN 1906

BRITANNIA 1917

MERCHANT ROYAL 1946

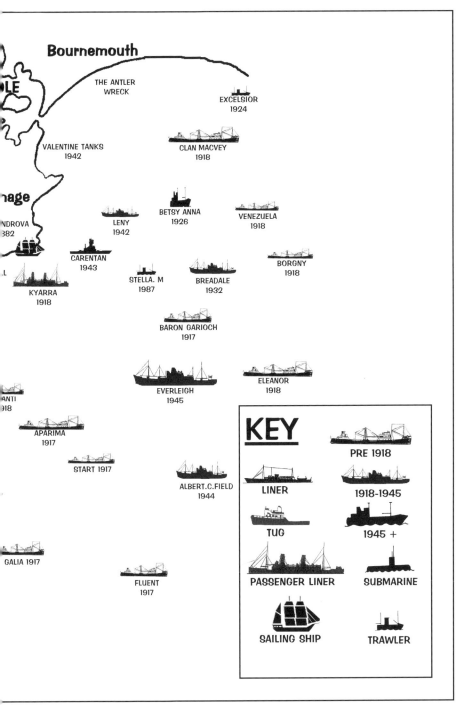

Bournemouth

OLE

THE ANTLER
WRECK

EXCELSIOR
1924

VALENTINE TANKS
1942

CLAN MACVEY
1918

nage

NDROVA
382

LENY
1942

BETSY ANNA
1926

VENEZUELA
1918

CARENTAN
1943

BORGNY
1918

L

STELLA. M
1987

BREADALE
1932

KYARRA
1918

BARON GARIOCH
1917

ANTI
018

EVERLEIGH
1945

ELEANOR
1918

APARIMA
1917

START 1917

ALBERT.C.FIELD
1944

GALIA 1917

FLUENT
1917

KEY

PRE 1918

LINER

1918-1945

TUG

1945 +

PASSENGER LINER

SUBMARINE

SAILING SHIP

TRAWLER

9

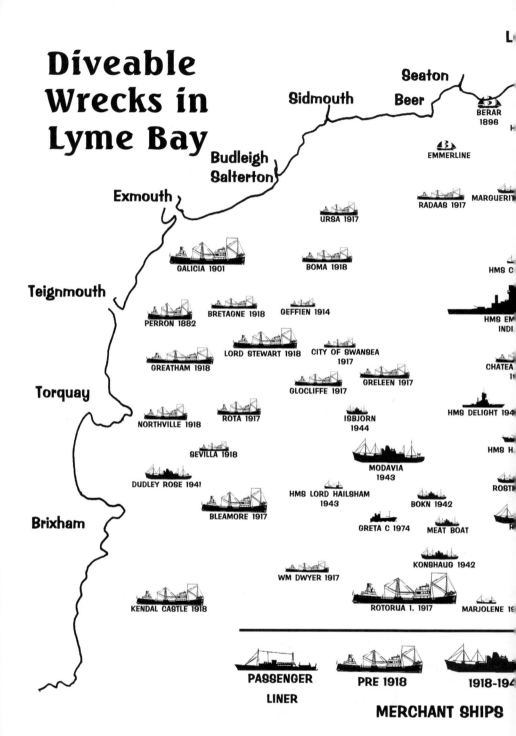

Diveable Wrecks in Lyme Bay

Seaton
Sidmouth   Beer
Budleigh Salterton
Exmouth
Teignmouth
Torquay
Brixham

BERAR 1896
EMMERLINE
MARGUERIT
RADAAS 1917
URSA 1917
GALICIA 1901
BOMA 1918
HMS C
PERRON 1882   BRETAGNE 1918   GEFFIEN 1914
HMS EM
INDI
LORD STEWART 1918   CITY OF SWANSEA 1917
GREATHAM 1918
CHATEA
GLOCLIFFE 1917   GRELEEN 1917
NORTHVILLE 1918   ROTA 1917
ISBJORN 1944
HMS DELIGHT 194
SEVILLA 1918
MODAVIA 1943
HMS H
DUDLEY ROSE 1941
HMS LORD HAILSHAM 1943
ROSTI
BLEAMORE 1917
BOKN 1942
GRETA C 1974   MEAT BOAT
R
KONSHAUG 1942
WM DWYER 1917
KENDAL CASTLE 1918
ROTORUA 1. 1917   MARJOLENE 19

PASSENGER LINER   PRE 1918   1918-194

MERCHANT SHIPS

10

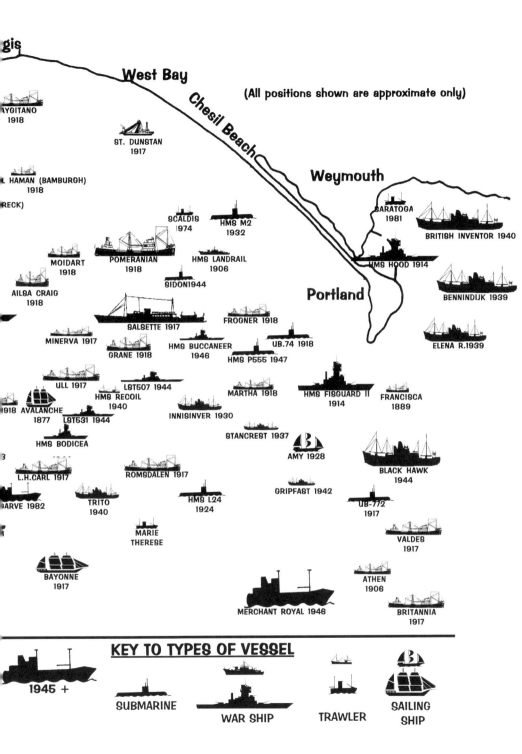

gis

West Bay

Chesil Beach

(All positions shown are approximate only)

AYGITANO
1918

ST. DUNSTAN
1917

L HAMAN (BAMBURGH)
1918

RECK)

Weymouth

SCALDIS
1974

HMS M2
1932

SARATOGA
1981

BRITISH INVENTOR 1940

MOIDART
1918

POMERANIAN
1918

HMS LANDRAIL
1906

HMS HOOD 1914

AILSA CRAIG
1918

SIDON 1944

BENNINDIJK 1939

Portland

MINERVA 1917

SALSETTE 1917

FROGNER 1918

ELENA R.1939

GRANE 1918

HMS BUCCANEER
1946

UB.74 1918

HMS P555 1947

ULL 1917

LST507 1944

HMS RECOIL
1940

MARTHA 1918

HMS FISGUARD II
1914

FRANCISCA
1889

1918 AVALANCHE
1877

LST531 1944

INNISINVER 1930

HMS BODICEA

STANCREST 1937

AMY 1928

L.H.CARL 1917

ROMSDALEN 1917

GRIPFAST 1942

BLACK HAWK
1944

ARVE 1982

TRITO
1940

HMS L24
1924

UB-772
1917

MARIE
THERESE

VALDES
1917

BAYONNE
1917

ATHEN
1906

MERCHANT ROYAL 1948

BRITANNIA
1917

KEY TO TYPES OF VESSEL

1945 +

SUBMARINE

WAR SHIP

TRAWLER

SAILING
SHIP

11

PORTLAND DIVING

In recent years, and with the departure of the Royal Navy, Portland has become one of the main centres for diving in the United Kingdom. There are several dive shops, and numerous boats offering charter both in the area and across to France and the Channel Islands.

The area can offer a dive in all weathers, either within the confines of the vast Portland Harbour or the sheltered coves, and even has that rare commodity – some free public launching slipways.

Portland Harbour

The building of this vast harbour was begun in 1849, and continued through to the completion of the north eastern arm in 1905. It was built to provide a base for the Royal Naval Channel Fleet. The rock was quarried from Portland, and nearly 6 million tons of stone was used; the harbour covers an area of 5,700 acres. Convicts supplied much of the labour.

In the 1980s the Naval base was deemed to be surplus to requirements, and sold to Portland Ports. The last naval presence left in 1999 with the closure of the helicopter-training base, though the Coastguard helicopter is still stationed there.

The commercial direction of the former harbour is not clear, and some of the wrecks require a permit to dive on, although charter boats have their own permits. For further details please contact the Harbour Master for the Port. (Tel. 01305 824044).

Launch Sites

There are slipways at Ferrybridge, Castletown, Weymouth Sailing Centre and Weymouth Harbour.

Shore Dives in the Portland Area (see Portland Map)

Newton's Cove: Depth 5-8 metres
Rocky ground best dived at high water.

Balaclava Bay – Grove Point Beaches:
Depth 12-30 metres
Rocky ledges with plenty of marine life. The tide near Grove Point can be strong.

Ferrybridge Underwater Nature Trail:
Depth 5-8 metres
Variety of marine life can be seen. Dive slack water one hour after Portland H/W.

Chesil Cove: Depth 12-18 metres
Large boulders and numerous bits of long lost wrecks can be found. There is little tide, though surf can make extrication from the sea difficult.

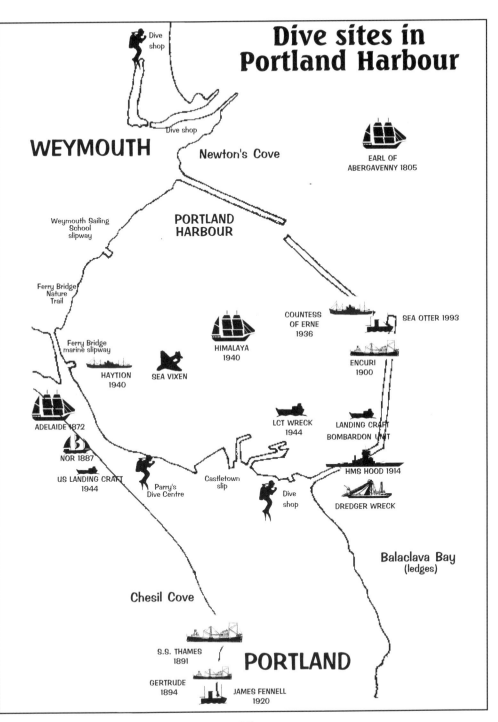

Dive sites in Portland Harbour

Dive shop

Dive shop

WEYMOUTH

Newton's Cove

EARL OF
ABERGAVENNY 1805

Weymouth Sailing
School
slipway

**PORTLAND
HARBOUR**

Ferry Bridge
Nature
Trail

COUNTESS
OF ERNE
1936

SEA OTTER 1993

Ferry Bridge
marine slipway

HIMALAYA
1940

ENCURI
1900

HAYTION
1940

SEA VIXEN

ADELAIDE 1872

LCT WRECK
1944

LANDING CRAFT
BOMBARDON UNIT

NOR 1887

US LANDING CRAFT
1944

Parry's
Dive Centre

Castletown
slip

Dive
shop

HMS HOOD 1914

DREDGER WRECK

Balaclava Bay
(ledges)

Chesil Cove

S.S. THAMES
1891

PORTLAND

GERTRUDE
1894

JAMES FENNELL
1920

13

LIST OF SHIPWRECKS THAT CAN BE DIVED OFF THE DORSET AND EAST DEVON COAST

AENEAS

TYPE	Passenger Liner
CARGO	General cargo – rubber and sandles
LENGTH	493ft
BEAM	60ft
DRAUGHT	27ft
DATE SUNK	1940.04.07
SEA DEPTH	56m

The liner was owned by Alfred Holt and Co and built in1910.

The ship was bombed and sunk by the Luftwaffe. After the war the Royal Navy used the wreck as a sonar target, and the ship was subject to regular depth-charge practice, which has destroyed most of the vessel. The ship was positively identified in the 1990s by divers operating from the Weymouth based boat Skin Deep, who are members of Lyme Bay Deep Divers and Kingston BSAC. To visit this wreck contact the dive boats operating out of Weymouth and Portland or contact Grahame Knott, skipper of Wey Chieftain II. Telephone 01305 771371.

AEOLIAN SKY

GPS	50 30.57N 02 08.42W
TYPE	Freighter (Greek)
TONNAGE	6,540
CARGO	Mixed cargo
LENGTH	148.74m
BEAM	21.95m
DRAUGHT	9.28m
DATE SUNK	1979.04.11
SEA DEPTH	30m

This large Greek freighter collided with another ship and was holed. Among the cargo manifest was £1.2 million in Seychelles currency. The wreck has been extensively salvaged and was reduced and cleared in 1980.The ship lies her port side and still contains a great deal of the cargo. The wreck is also famous for the number of Marmite jars and perfume bottles it contains. There are also Landrovers and Range Rovers as part of the cargo.

The Aeolian Sky is one of the most recent wrecks off the Dorset coast. She was a general cargo carrier bound from London to Nigeria, among the cargo were trains, Range Rovers, Landrovers, cloth and a large sum of Mauritius Rupees.

While sailing down the English Channel she collided with the Anna Knueppal, a German registered ship of 1,000 tons. The Aeolian Sky was holed and leaking. The Captain tried to make for the nearest harbour but sank 12 miles east of Portland the followingt day. The Anna Knueppel was not badly damaged and was able to make port.

The Government issued a warning that the vessel, The Aeolian Sky, was carrying dangerous unspecified chemicals. This would seem to have been a ploy to keep divers off the wreck, till the salvage could start to recover the goods and the large sum of Mauritius money. When salvage divers entered the ship they found the money had already gone from the safe.

The ship has since been extensively salvaged. Her propellers were brought up in 1980. The navy demolished some of the top structure, as it was a hazard to shipping.

AILSA CRAIG

GPS	50 33.68N 02 47.54W
TYPE	Steamship (armed)
TONNAGE	601
CARGO	Coal
LENGTH	184ft
BEAM	28ft
DRAUGHT	11ft
DATE SUNK	1918.15.04
SEA DEPTH	33m

The Ailsa Craig was an armed British steamer en route from Cardiff to Weymouth with a cargo of coal. The ship carried a stern gun, which has been recovered, and also ammunition. The wreck is now privately owned and is a popular dive. The sea bedis of fine sediment, which is easily disturbed. The wreck can be reached from boats operating from West Bay or Lyme Regis.

15

ALBERT C FIELD

GPS	50 28.24N 01 45.35W
TYPE	Steamship
TONNAGE	1,764
CARGO	Ammunition
LENGTH	252ft
DATE SUNK	1944.18.06
SEA DEPTH	38m

The British government requisitioned the steamship for the war. She was armed with two Hotchkiss machine guns. The ship was a general cargo carrier. The Albert. C. Field was attacked and sunk by German aircraft, towards the end of WW2. She was carrying a large quantity of ammunition, which exploded after the attack. The vessel broke up and now lies off Anvil Point.

ALEX VAN OPSTAL

GPS	50 32.43N 02 16.03W
TYPE	Passenger liner (Belgium)
TONNAGE	5,964
CARGO	General
LENGTH	420ft
DATES SUNK	1939.15.09
SEA DEPTH	30m

Ship sank after hitting a mine. The bow section is intact and stands 7m clear of a gravel seabed. The stern is very broken up. The wreck now lies seven and a half miles ENE, off Portland Bill. The Opstal is a recommended wreck for the novice diver. A safe and interesting dive.

ALEXANDROVA

GPS	50 35.43N 01 58.00W
TYPE	Sailing
TONNAGE	1,250
CARGO	Cotton

DATE SUNK   1882.29.04

The sailing vessel, Alexandrova, was driven onto rocks during a severe storm. She struck the cliffs half a mile from Swanage lighthouse. All crew and passengers perished. There is little left of this wreck.

ALGARVE

GPS	50 22.81N 02 48.51W
TYPE	Steamship (armed)
TONNAGE	1,214
LENGTH	229ft
BEAM	34ft
DRAUGHT	15ft
DATE SUNK	1917.20.10
SEA DEPTH	51m

The Algarve was torpedoed, killing twenty of the crew. The Algarve was only identified in 1996. She lies about 15 miles WSW off Portland Bill. There are still some doubts about the identity of this wreck.

AMY

GPS	50 26.43N 02 31.20W
TYPE	Sailing (Schooner)
TONNAGE	230
DATE SUNK	1928.15.03
SEA DEPTH	46m

The Amy was a failed film star that sank during the making of a film about Q-ships. A Q-ship was a heavily armed camouflaged merchantmen or trawler, that were used in WW1 to entice German submarines to attack. The Q-ship carefully hid its guns and weaponry till it was possible to attack the U-boat. How this vessel came to sink is a mystery.

ANTLER WRECK

GPS	50 40.46N 01 55.41W
TYPE	Barge/Coaster

CARGO	Deer antlers and stone
SEA DEPTH	7m

The wreck has not been positively identified and could be two wrecks. Recovered goods included blocks of stone and deer antlers (sometimes used as knife handles). There is an opinion that this could be the debris of two wrecks from different periods, which lie next to each other.

ANTONIS G LEMOS

TYPE	Steamship (Greek)
TONNAGE	4,410
LENGTH	385ft
BEAM	52ft
DRAUGHT	25ft
DATE SUNK	1936.24.08
SEA DEPTH	62m (scour of 70m)

The Lemos sank after a collision with HMS Keith. The ship stands 16 metres above the seabed. It is located about 30 miles south of Portland Bill. There are doubts over the identity of this wreck. Local Weymouth skipper, Grahame Knott, reckons that this large collier is probably an earlier ship, than the Lemos. The bows of the wreck are blown off and there is a large scour to 70 metres. Locally known as the Black Wreck, it is dived by Weymouth and Portland based boats.

ANWORTH

GPS	50 31.58N 02 33.70W
TYPE	Steamship
LENGTH	150ft
SEA DEPTH	38m

The Anworth, has not been positively identified. The wreck rises 8 metres off the seabed, and the stern is broken up. The hold contains bags of cement. The bell has been recovered. The wreck is about 18 miles from Lyme Regis. There is no record for the sinking of this vessel in this area or a ship with this name. The name on the bell is a mystery!

APARIMA

GPS	50 29.46N 01 54.96W
TYPE	Liner
TONNAGE	5,704
LENGTH	430ft
DATE SUNK	1917.19.11
SEA DEPTH	42m

The Aparima had triple expansion engines, and was built in Scotland for the general passenger and cargo trade between New Zealand and Australia. The British government in 1917 requisitioned the ship. The Aparima was attacked and torpedoed by U-boat 40. She lies upright on the sea bedabout 6 miles off Anvil Point.

ATHEN

GPS	50 20.71N 02 27.72W
TYPE	Steamship
TONNAGE	2,199
CARGO	Coal (Patent crushed bricks)
LENGTH	228ft
BEAM	38ft
DRAUGHT	19ft
DATE SUNK	1906.19.02
SEA DEPTH	53m

The Athen sank after a mid-channel collision with the SS Thoren while en route from Cardiff. The wreck lies upright and the hull is intact. The wreck has been positively identified.

AVALANCHE

GPS	50 26.56N 02 50.66W
TYPE	Sailing (iron clad)
TONNAGE	1,210
CARGO	General cargo
LENGTH	215ft

BEAM	36ft
DRAUGHT	21ft
DATE SUNK	1877.11.09
SEA DEPTH	50m

The Avalanche was on passage from London to New Zealand when it collided with another ship, The Forest, (1,244 ton sailing vessel). The Avalanche suffered a large gash in the hull, which caused the ship to sink within ten minutes of the accident, leaving little time for the passengers to evacuate the stricken vessel.

On board were a total of 93 crew and passengers; only three survived the catastrophe. The wreck of the Avalanche was discovered in 1984 and a large number of objects have been recovered. Part of the salvage collection can be seen at the Maritime section of Weymouth museum at Brewers' Quay. The vessel lies upside down.

Sailors are superstitious and more so in the days of sail, when it was the power of the wind that dictated your departure, journey and arrival. It was not a good omen to the crew of the Avalanche when she lost her figurehead at the start of the voyage, in a collision with a barge, while sailing down the Thames.

The Avalanche was bound for New Zealand, with a crew of thirty-four, and sixty-four passengers. The Avalanche was iron built, and carried a general cargo of goods worth in total £100,000.

On Tuesday the 11th September, a few miles off Portland, the weather was raining with mist. The watch spotted lights from the bridge, it was the S.S. Forest, a Canadian registered sailing vessel, in ballast with a crew of 21. The two ships were on opposite tacks. The Forest on a starboard tack had right of way, and burnt flares to warn the Avalanche of his approach. It was to no avail, neither Captain took evasive courses.

The Forest struck the Avalanche amidships, rebounding from the first impact under full sail she drove once more into the stern of the Avalanche. The Avalanche with large gashes in her side sank quickly.

All on board the Avalanche were drowned, except for the 3rd mates and two Seamen, who scrambled from the Avalanche onto the Forest, during the collision.

The Forest was also damaged and started to ship water through a. large hole in the bow. Captain Lockhart ordered the crew to abandon ship. The three lifeboats were launched, though some of the crew in the confusion were left on board. Of the three boats, only one reached the safety of Portland. The collision was a disaster and 102 people were lost.

A memorial Church was built to the victims at Southwell Cliff Portland, from donations sent in by the public.

AVANTI

GPS	50 29.82N 01 55.05W
TYPE	Steamship
TONNAGE	2,128
LENGTH	272ft
BEAM	40ft
DRAUGHT	21ft
DATE SUNK	1918.02.02
SEA DEPTH	46m

The Avanti was torpedoed while en route from Bilbao with 3,500 tons of iron ore. The wreck is very broken up and the highest point is 6m off the sea floor. The Avanti lies on the sea bed about 4 miles off Anvil Point on the East Dorset coast. The wreck is inverted.

AXMOUTH WRECK

GPS	253 901 OS map ref 192
TYPE	Medieval
DATE SUNK	14th century
SEA DEPTH	1m

A local boat builder, Paul Mears, discovered this interesting wreck in December 2001. A new bridge had changed the flow of the river Axe uncovering some old timbers. The wood was pegged with no iron nails. Paul recognised the antiquity of the build and notified the archaeological centre in Exeter. Subsequent tree dating of a sample identified the wreck as possibly 14th century. Axmouth is a very ancient port dating back to the Roman occupation of Britain. The river silted up and the trade and port declined.

BAMBURGH see GIBAL HAMAM

BAMSE

GPS	50 26.25N 02 53.54W
TYPE	Steamship (Norwegian)
TONNAGE	985

CARGO	Ballast
LENGTH	223ft
BEAM	30ft
DRAUGHT	16ft
DATE SUNK	1918.17.04
SEA DEPTH	48m

The ship was on passage from Rouen for Swansea when attacked and torpedoed. The wreck is very broken up and lies 18 miles off Lyme Regis. The wreck has not been positively identified.

BARMSTON

GPS	50 32.66N 02 27.39W
TYPE	Steamship
TONNAGE	1,431
CARGO	Coal
LENGTH	76.20m
BEAM	10.82m
DRAUGHT	4.88m
DATE SUNK	1918.21.03
SEA DEPTH	16m

Ran aground under Blacknor Point while on passage from Swansea to northern France.

BARON GARIOCH

GPS	50 31.34N 01 45.82W
TYPE	Steamship
TONNAGE	1,831
CARGO	Ballast
LENGTH	265ft
BEAM	37ft
DATE SUNK	1917.28.10
SEA DEPTH	38m

Torpedoed while en route from Calais to Liverpool after delivering supplies for the fighting in northern France, during WW1. Ship's bell has been discovered. The wreck lies 5 miles off Anvil Point.

BAYGITANO (Ex Cayo Gitano)

GPS	50 41.78N 02 56.07W
TYPE	Steamship (armed) Great Lakes Trader. Built 1905
TONNAGE	3,073
CARGO	Ballast
LENGTH	331ft
BEAM	45ft
DRAUGHT	16ft
DATE SUNK	1918.18.03
SEA DEPTH	17m

The wreck lies 1.5 miles from Lyme Regis and is one of the most popular to dive on the Dorset coast. The ship was torpedoed during the First World War, with the loss of two of the crew. The U-boat (U-77) captain then surfaced to ascertain which boat he had sunk. The Lyme Regis lifeboat rescued the remaining crew. The wreck is broken up, though the bows and engines can be found very easily, and the boilers rise up and are very distinct. The wreck has been salvaged. The bows lie to the west. It hosts diverse marine life, and although it is fished all year, this does not seem to affect the large numbers of fish that can be seen. The mast lies off at an angle from the wreck, and is occasionally inhabited by a large conger eel. Boats regularly take out divers and anglers to the wreck from Lyme Regis.

An eldery resident described an eyewitness account of the sinking of the Baygitano, the transcripts of which are at Lyme Regis Museum.

"I got home the night before the sinking, while on leave. I was having a lie in when I heard a loud explosion. Looking out of the window I saw one of the fishermen running past, pulling on his sea-jersey." "What is it Frank?" I said, "A ship has been torpedoed off the Cobb." So I went down to the harbour, it was coming in thick fog. The lifeboat went out with a scratch crew. The lifeboat crew took their jumpers off, so that they wouldn't look like a naval boat. It was a lovely flat calm sea. The rowing boats went out and brought the crew in. The submarine surfaced and talked to the rowing boats, and asked where the captain of the torpedoed vessel was. He happened to be in the boat they spoke to. So they said, he was in one of the boats that had gone ashore. The submarine

23

Captain wanted to know the name of the ship, which he had sunk.

Another witness described the large number of people on the Cobb watching the incident, and that after the sinking only the masts protruded above the water."

BAYONNE

GPS	50 15.490N 02 50.14W
TYPE	Sailing Vessel (French steel)
TONNAGE	2,589 (built 1901)
CARGO	Maize and barley
LENGTH	283ft
BEAM	44ft
DRAUGHT	23ft
DATE SUNK	1917.17.02
SEA DEPTH	61m

The Bayonne sank while en route from New York to Ipswich. The vessel lies upright. The identity of this wreck has not been confirmed.

BENNY'S WRECK see MARGUERITE

BERAR

GPS	50 41.90N 03 00.29W. (Charton Bay between Lyme Regis and Seaton)
TYPE	Sailing barque
CARGO	Sawn timber (salvaged)
DATE SUNK	1896.07.10

This sailing ship was holed and foundered when sailing to close to the shore in foggy conditions. The wreck lies just off Culverhole Point. The Berar was carrying a cargo of sawn timber and marble. The timber was salvaged by the construction of a raft and kedged back to the near-by harbour at Axmouth. You can walk out to the wreck at low tide, when the ribs and keel are exposed. The wreck is on the rocky ledges near Charlton Bay at the western part. There is a lot of kelp, and it makes a good snorkel dive. In August 2001, Dr Glanville found some brass on the bow area, which he was unable to free. There is a debris field running onto the beach. The wreck was extensively salvaged at the turn of the century. On the beach are the remains of a trawler, the Fairway, and an abandoned digger, drowned in the attempts to salvage the Fairway.

BENNINDIJK (BENNY)

GPS	50 32.11N 02 20.01W
TYPE	Freighter (Dutch)
TONNAGE	6,873
CARGO	Oil and general cargo
LENGTH	400ft
BEAM	54ft
DATE SUNK	1939.08.09
SEA DEPTH	27m

The wreck is very broken up and has been extensively salvaged. The vessel sank after hitting a mine. The dive can only be undertaken during slack water. Visibility is often restricted on the site due to the nearby Admant Shoal and Shambles Bank.

BETSY ANNA

GPS	50 37.00N 01 48.84W
TYPE	Coaster
TONNAGE	880
CARGO	Ballast
LENGTH	63m
BEAM	9.17m
DRAUGHT	4.29m
DATE SUNK	1926.17.08
SEA DEPTH	24m

The vessel foundered while under tow. The Betsy Anna had sustained damage off the Devon coast. The bow has collapsed and the wreck stands 5metres above the seabed.

BLACK HAWK

BLACK HAWK (bow)

GPS	50 36.68N 02 12.43W
TYPE	Steamship (Liberty ship)
DATE SUNK	1944.12.07

The bow section was towed to Worbarrow Bay. In 1967 it was blown up to make way for a cooling pipe for Winfrith. Debris litters the sea bedas a result of the demolition charges.

BLACK HAWK (stern)

GPS	50 26.17N 02 25.30W
TYPE	Steamship (Liberty ship)
LENGTH	441ft
BEAM	57ft
DRAUGHT	35ft
SEA DEPTH	50m

The ship was torpedoed and the stern was broken off after the attack. The forepart of the ship was salvaged and towed to Worbarrow Bay where the rusting hulk remained till 1967 when it was blown up and removed to make way for a cooling pipeline for the nearby nuclear power station at Winfrith. Shell cases and ordnance have been found on the site of the stern. The wreck rises 10 metres off the seabed.

BLEAMOOR

GPS	50 22.73N 03 25.32W
TYPE	Steamship (turret deck)
TONNAGE	3,755
CARGO	Coal
LENGTH	342ft
BEAM	47ft
DRAUGHT	25ft
DATE SUNK	1917.27.11
SEA DEPTH	44m

The wreck lies upside down, east to west and is very broken up. The highest point of the wreck is 7 metres clear of the bottom.

BOKN

GPS	50 22.00N 02 59.01W
TYPE	Steamship (Norwegian)
TONNAGE	698
LENGTH	193ft
BEAM	28ft
DRAUGHT	11ft
DATE SUNK	1942.09.07
SEA DEPTH	55m

The ship was torpedoed and sunk by German gunboats. The wreck lies upright but is very broken up. The stern section is reasonably intact but ends at the boiler section. The wreck could be in two pieces. The winch and hold are aft of the engine. The identity has not been confirmed.

BOMA

GPS	50 32.186N 03 14.286W
TYPE	Steamship
TONNAGE	2,694
CARGO	Potatoes, hay and straw

LENGTH	312ft
BEAM	39ft
DRAUGHT	25ft
DATE SUNK	1918.11.06
SEA DEPTH	28m

The ship was torpedoed by the German U-boat 80. The Boma was extensively salvaged during the 1970s. The wreck lies on fine sand and visibility is often poor. There are lots of fish on this wreck. The wreck is infrequently dived though visitors should beware of drifting bass fishing boats on the surface.

BOMBARDON UNIT

GPS	50 37.53N 02 24.17W
TYPE	Concrete breakwater
DATE SUNK	1944
SEA DEPTH	15m

In Portland Harbour (see map for details) The Bombardon Unit was an experimental floating wave-breaking barge, which was star shaped. There are lots of hatches and girders. The wreck lies on a silt bed. Nearby, is a second barge with its rudder and propellers intact.

The bombardon units were part of the structure of the Mulberry Harbour which were constructed so that the units could be floated across the English Channel and re-assembled to provide a floating harbour for the logistical support of the armies at the start of the D-Day landings in 1944. The harbour was made from prefabricated concrete units, which were towed across to France and slotted together like a giant jigsaw. The sea could have easily destroyed such a large structure and Dr F.H.Todd was tasked with finding a design for breaking up the waves. He tested numerous designs and models at the large indoor water tanks at the Hydraulics Research centre at Teddington and eventually implemented a plan for two floating breakwaters known as bombardons. They constructed over six miles of these units to protect the harbour. Valves were incorporated into the design to adjust the buoyancy. The two units in Portland Harbour are part of this elaborate historic construction. We believe that this unit failed to make the trip!

BORGA (See NYASALAND)

TYPE	Steamship
TONNAGE	1,046
CARGO	Coal
LENGTH	229ft
BEAM	35ft
DRAUGHT	16ft
DATE SUNK	1918.01.03
SEA DEPTH	55m

Although this vessel is said to be the Borga, measurements of this ship suggest otherwise. It is possible that the wreck is in fact that of the Nyasaland.

BORGNY

GPS	50 35.44N 01 41.64W
TYPE	Steamship
TONNAGE	1,149
CARGO	Coal 1,500 tons
LENGTH	228ft
BEAM	36ft
DATE SUNK	1918.22.02
SEA DEPTH	27m

The cause of the sinking is unknown. The wreck is well broken up and rises 5 metres above the sea floor. The sea bed is sand and gravel. The wreck has been positively identified.

BORGUND 1

GPS	50 26.15N 03 03.51W
TYPE	Steamship
TONNAGE	763
CARGO	Coal
LENGTH	195ft

BEAM	30ft
DRAUGHT	14ft
DATE SUNK	1917.30.06
SEA DEPTH	52m

The Borgund has not been positively identified. There is confusion between the Lloyds loss chart position and that shown above. The vessel rounded Start point at 5.30 a.m. in a strong NE wind. She was sunk three hours later in a position WNW of Portland Bill. The wreck is very broken up and collapsed.

BRAEDALE

GPS	50 33.38N 01 45.34W
TYPE	Steamship
TONNAGE	406
CARGO	Apples
LENGTH	142ft
BEAM	25ft
DATE SUNK	1932.16.10
SEA DEPTH	33m

The Braedale was built in 1892. She sank while en route from Dieppe to Bristol in heavy weather when water entered her holds.

BRETAGNE

GPS (bow)	50 29.479N 03 22.691W
GPS (stern)	50 29.503N 03 22.688W
TYPE	Sailing (Schooner rigged steamship)
TONNAGE	1,888
CARGO	Coal
LENGTH	232ft
BEAM	35ft
DRAUGHT	15ft
DATE SUNK	1918.10.08
SEA DEPTH	29m

The ship was en route from Barry to Rouen when she collided in thick fog with another vessel. She remained afloat and salvage was attempted but the Bretagne sank while under tow. The stern gun is still in place, and the holds still contain coal. The wreck is in good condition and interesting to dive. Recommended by local divers. You can go inside the wreck and it is regularly dived by South West Divers (telephone 01395 268090). One of the most popular dived wrecks in Lyme Bay.

BRITANNIA

GPS	50 20.31N 02 26.71W
TYPE	Steamship
TONNAGE	3,028
CARGO	Animals and cattle and general cargo
LENGTH	300ft
BEAM	40ft
DRAUGHT	28ft
DATE SUNK	1884.31.07
SEA DEPTH	56m

She collided with another ship and sank. The wreck is very broken up and the engine lies on its starboard side.

BRITISH INVENTOR

GPS	50 35.40N 02 18.36W
TYPE	Tanker (oil)
TONNAGE	7,101
CARGO	Diesel and kerosene
LENGTH	131.07m
BEAM	17.71m
DRAUGHT	10.36m
DATE SUNK	1940.13.06
SEA DEPTH	18m

The ship struck a sea mine, though only the bow sank, and the stern was salvaged. The highest point is only 2metres above the seabed. The bow section is lying on the seabed. The wreck lies near Lulworth Banks and divers should be aware of the strong tides in this area.

The British Inventor was a victim of a sea mine, on the 13th of June 1940. She struck the mine in calm waters. Disabled she floated towards the shambles. The lifeboat was launched from Portland, though first on the scenes was armed naval yacht which managed to take off the twenty-five crew. The British Inventor was still afloat and Admiralty tugs tried in vain to tow her into Portland, but by late afternoon the tanker had taken in too much water and she foundered and sank.

BROOMHILL

GPS	50 27.61N 02 48.85W
TYPE	Collier
TONNAGE	1,392
CARGO	Coal 1,700tons
LENGTH	243ft
BEAM	36ft
DRAUGHT	15ft
DATE SUNK	1917.10.05
SEA DEPTH	50m

The Broomhill was scuttled after the ship was attacked and captured by a German U-boat. The initial gunfire from the submarine killed two of the crew. The ship lies on her side and has been tentatively identified by Lyme Bay Deep Divers. The wreck rests on the sea bed with the stern section to the south. The propeller has been salvaged. The wreck lies about 9 miles southwest of Portland Bill.

BUESTEN

GPS	50 21.38N 03 24.47W
TYPE	Tanker
TONNAGE	5,187
CARGO	Benzene and Kerosene
LENGTH	118.29m
BEAM	16.06m
DRAUGHT	8.4m
DATE SUNK	1941.09.04
SEA DEPTH	50m

The Norwegian owned ship was bombed by the Luftwaffe. The attack killed 28 of the crew. The wreck lies on its starboard side and the deck is vertical. The bows are to the east.

CARENTAN

GPS	50 34.96N 01 56.16W
TYPE	Warship (Anti submarine)
TONNAGE	135
LENGTH	121ft
DATE SUNK	1943.19.12

The Carentan foundered during a storm.

CASTLE REAGH

GPS	50 34 83N 01 56 10W
TYPE	Coaster
CARGO	Coal
LENGTH	168ft
DATE SUNK	1925.25.02
SEA DEPTH	37m

The bell has been confirmed. The ship was reported overdue, and the bodies of some of the crew were found one week later. The top structure of the wreck is missing but much of the hull is intact. The bows stand 6 metres clear of the seabed.

CHASSEUR

GPS	50 25.46N 02 04.84W
TYPE	Warship (Anti submarine)
DATE SUNK	1940.12.10
SEA DEPTH	40m

The Chasseur was sunk by German naval gunfire when it sailed into the path of a German patrol. The wreck lies upright on the seabed, and in recent years portholes and some brass fittings have been salvaged from the vessel; there is also a quantity of unexploded ordnance. The Chasseur was only discovered in 1996.

CHATEAU YQUEM

GPS	50 29.11N 02 58.97W
TYPE	Steamship
TONNAGE	1,913
LENGTH	280ft
BEAM	38ft
DRAUGHT	21.4ft
DATE SUNK	1917.17.04
SEA DEPTH	48m

The steamship attacked and torpedoed by the German submarine U-40. The bow and stern are intact, although the wreck has some superstructure missing including the wheelhouse and some of the top structure. The telegraph has been recovered and the wreck has been positively identified. This wreck is recommended as an interesting dive and the vessel is in good condition and intact.

CHORLEY

GPS	50 19.069N 03 03 47.5W
TYPE	Steamship
TONNAGE	3,828
LENGTH	160ft
DATE SUNK	1917.22.03
SEA DEPTH	61m

The Chorley was attacked by the German submarine U-48.The wreck is almost intact and rises 9metres off the seabed.

CITY OF SWANSEA

GPS	50 28.85N 03 11.44W
TYPE	Steamship
TONNAGE	1,375
CARGO	Coal 1,682 tons
LENGTH	260ft
BEAM	35ft

DRAUGHT   16ft

DATE SUNK   1917.25.09

SEA DEPTH   39m

The ship was torpedoed and lies on her port side. The stern section has broken away from the main vessel.

CLAN MACVEY

GPS   50 39.65N 01 46.72W

TYPE   Steamship

TONNAGE   5,815

CARGO   Coal

LENGTH   400ft

BEAM   53ft

DRAUGHT   32ft

DATE SUNK   1918.08.08

SEA DEPTH   18m

The Clan Macvey was torpedoed and sank while under tow, after an earlier attack, which has disabled the ship. The wreck is very broken up and lies on fine sand.

COUNTESS OF ERNE

GPS   50 35.18N 02 25.19W

TYPE   Paddle steamer

TONNAGE   900

LENGTH   240ft

BEAM   30ft

DATE SUNK   1935.16.09

SEA DEPTH   14m

The steamer had been converted into a coal hulk and sank after breaking her mooring. She broke up on the inner side of the North Breakwater. Sea bedis silt and much of the superstructure has been demolished. The wreck lies upright and can be dived at any stage of the tide. Local divers recommend this wreck as ideal for novice divers.

DAGMAR

GPS	50 28.00N 02 01.85W
TYPE	Collier
TONNAGE	2,471
CARGO	Oranges coal
LENGTH	88.55m
BEAM	09.02m
DATE SUNK	1941.09.06
SEA DEPTH	42m

The Dagmar sank after being bombed while en route from Wales to Poole.

DERNA

GPS	50 27.27N 02 00.20W
TYPE	Steamship (tramp)
TONNAGE	2,210
DATE SUNK	1912
SEA DEPTH	42m

The ship sank after a collision with HMS Centurion, a dreadnought class battleship. The wreck is very broken up.

DIVER TRAINING WRECK (see The Greatham)

GPS	50.17.971N 03.30.519W
TYPE	Steamship
SEA_DEPTH	42m

This is probably the wreck of the Greatham. The wreck is cut in half in front of the bridge. The chronometer and telegraph have been recovered, although there has been no positive identification. There is a deep scour around the wreck. The wreck was named because local boat owners once saw divers on the wreck and called it the Diver Training Wreck.

DREDGER WRECK

GPS	50 34.03N 02 25.45W (off Portland)
TYPE	Dredger
SEA DEPTH	6-12m

This old sand dredger is very broken up. The bottom is sandy and the tide here is not a problem. The vessel lies in two parts: one section of 12metres and the other 6metres. The wreck is often buoyed and lies parallel to the sea wall.

DUDLEY ROSE

GPS	50 23.65N 03 26.24W
TYPE	Collier
TONNAGE	1,600
CARGO	Coal
LENGTH	250ft
DATE SUNK	1941.09.0
SEA DEPTH	37m

The Dudley Rose was bombed by the Luftwaffe and sunk. The wreck lies upright and rises 10metres above the seabed. Visibility is normally poor on this site. The wreck is largely intact and an interesting dive. Visitors should be aware of a number of discarded fishing nets that are attached to this wreck.

EARL OF ABERGAVENNY

GPS	50 36.13N 02 24.50W
TYPE	Sailing (East Indiaman)
TONNAGE	1,200
CARGO	General, gold and silver, personal items
DATE SUNK	1805.05.02
SEA DEPTH	18m

The East Indiaman was captained by John Wordsworth, brother of the famous poet, and was en route for India. The vessel ran into the Shambles and became stuck. A small boat came out from Portland and took off 3 men and 2 women and a further 60 passengers were rescued as the weather deteriorated. Over 270 crew and passengers perished in the sinking. The wreck is about 1.5 miles SE of the harbour entrance. The wreck is covered in mud and there has been an archaeological dig on the site. You can still see some of the timbers and find musket flints. The meticulous uncovering of this wreck and the numerous finds are shown on a web site at (www.weymouthdiving.co.uk). There is also a book about the wreck, by

Ed Cummins, who is one of the divers leading the archaeological dig. This is one of the most researched sites on the Dorset coast and it is well worth looking at the web site.

Earl of Abergavenny

One of the most tragic sinking off the Dorset coast was the Loss of the Earl of Abergavenny. The Abergavenny was an East Indiaman of 1,200 imperial tons. Her captain was John Wordsworth, the brother of the poet William Wordsworth.

The ship left Portsmouth on February 1st 1805 bound for India and China. A trading mission which, if successful, would have made John Wordsworth and his backers a healthy profit. The ship carried a large cargo and over 400 passengers and crew, including 160 new recruits for the East India Company army, thirty Chinese and sixty ordinary passengers.

The Earl of Abergavenny set out in convoy with four other vessels. During the voyage the weather deteriorated and the ships sought shelter behind Portland. While sheltering, the Abergavenny drifted onto the Shambles. The wind had died, and there was no danger. Captain Wordsworth waited for the tide to float him free. The wind increased and the Abergavenny pounded the bottom. The ships carpenter found a leak in one of the holds, which soon filled with water, despite desperate pumping. The ship settled back onto the sand of the shambles. There was still no immediate danger as the sea was still moderate. The Captain sent the purser ashore, with the ships papers; two lady passengers and six crew to go and seek aid for the stricken ship. On board the Abergavenny the sailors were encouraged to man the pumps by a free issue of grog, It was not till 9.00 p.m. that the passengers were told of the predicament. By then, the weather had worsened considerably and there was little hope of using the ships lifeboats. At 11 p.m. the ship sank, many were drowned in the icy winter waters, others climbed into the rigging, which rose out of the sea. It was not until an hour later that any rescue was attempted. A local sloop came close and rescued many who clung to the spars and ropes. By daybreak, the full extent of the tragedy was revealed. Two hundred and thirty three people had drowned; Captain Wordsworth also went down with his ship, his body being recovered a month later on the beach at Weymouth. The local beaches were covered with the

38

clothes and remains of the ship. The bodies of many that were drowned were buried in a mass grave at Wyke Regis. Salvage attempts were made to rescue the cargo, which were only partially successful.

ELEANOR

GPS	50 30.11N 01 40.35W
TYPE	Steamship
TONNAGE	1,980
CARGO	Mines, depth charges, ordnance
LENGTH	82.30m
BEAM	10.97m
DRAUGHT	6.10m
DATE SUNK	1918.12.02
SEA DEPTH	39m

The ship was built in 1888 with a three-cylinder triple expansion engine. The ship was attacked and sunk by the German submarine U-57, which caused the death of 34 of the crew, while en route from Immingham to Falmouth. There is still a large quantity of ordnance on this wreck.

ELENA R

GPS	50 30.19N 02 20.66W
TYPE	Steamship (Greek)
TONNAGE	4576
CARGO	Grain
LENGTH	370ft
BEAM	53.4ft
DRAUGHT	7ft
DATE SUNK	1939.22.11
SEA DEPTH	27m

The ship was mined and is located off the Shambles about 8 miles from Weymouth. The wreck is very broken up. The shingle banks and sands of the Shambles cover parts of the wreckage. Beware of the strong tides in this area. The highest part of the wreck stands 8 metres from the sea bed.

ELSA (Greatham)

GPS	50 18.25N 03 30.32W
TYPE	Steamship (freighter)
TONNAGE	2,338
CARGO	Coal
LENGTH	290ft
BEAM	38ft
DATE SUNK	1918.22.01
SEA DEPTH	44m

The wreck was originally known as the Greatham. She was attacked by the German submarine U-91. Recent research by Simon Bussett, a local diver who measured the wreck, suggests that this is not the Greatham, but is probably the wreck of the Elsa. The wreck lies upright. The highest point of the ship is 6 metres clear of the seabed. The beam measurement does not conform to that of the Greatham, this wreck is 10ft too wide. The Greatham is probably the wreck off Dartmouth called the Diver Training Wreck, although neither wreck has been positively identified.

EMMERLINE

GPS	50 38.13W 03 05.47W
TYPE	Sailing Ship

There is very little left of this vessel.

ENECURI (The Spaniard)

GPS	50 34.81N 02 24.92W
TYPE	Steamship (Spanish)
TONNAGE	2,385
CARGO	Ballast
LENGTH	87.54m
BEAM	12.16m
DRAUGHT	5.73m
DATE SUNK	1900.29.12
SEA DEPTH	12m

The Enecuri dragged her anchor during a southwest gale and was driven onto the breakwater in Portland Harbour. The wreck is now just a tangled mass of broken plates. The crew of 26 were saved from the disaster, but the captain and his dog went down with the ship.

ETHEL

GPS	50 28.37N 02 20.87W
TYPE	Steamship
TONNAGE	2,336
CARGO	Ballast
LENGTH	88.39m
BEAM	12.80m
DRAUGHT	5.18m
DATE SUNK	1918.16.09
SEA DEPTH	35m

The Ethel is now very broken up and lies on sand and shingle. The bows are detached from the main part of the ship. The Ethel sank while under tow after being torpedoed by the German submarine U-104.

During the Second World War, Portland was a designated salvage recovery port; floating and damaged vessels were towed to the large harbour for later attempts at salvage.

EVERLEIGH

GPS	50 29.30N 01 47.10W	
TYPE	Steamship	
TONNAGE	5,222	
CARGO	Ballast	
LENGTH	406ft	
BEAM	56ft	
DRAUGHT	27ft	
DATE SUNK	1945.06.02	
SEA DEPTH	40m	

The Everleigh was one of the last vessels sunk off the Dorset coast at the end of WW2. She was on passage from London to New York when

41

attacked and torpedoed by a German submarine. The wreck rises 11metres off the seabed. The ship was armed with a 4-inch gun and ammunition has been found on the wreck. The wreck now lies on her port side and is about 14 miles from Poole Harbour.

EVERTSEN

GPS	50 22.89N 02 13.61W
TYPE	Motor Vessel (Dutch)
TONNAGE	392
CARGO	China clay
LENGTH	56.36m
BEAM	9.11m
DRAUGHT	3.63m
DATE SUNK	1961.24.06
SEA DEPTH	48m

The Evertsen collided with another vessel during thick fog, south of Portland Bill, while en route from Par, in Cornwall to Rotterdam. She was loaded with a cargo of China clay. She sank within two hours of the accident.

EXCELSIOR

GPS	50 40.41N 01 44.80W
TYPE	Trawler (Fishing Drifter)
CARGO	Scrap metal
DATE SUNK	1924.05.09
SEA DEPTH	19m

Known locally as the Pipe Wreck due to the number of pipes to be found around the wreck. This was probably the cargo. The Excelsior sprang a leak and foundered while en route from Portsmouth to Newport. The boiler stands proud of the wreck.

FINN

GPS	50 13.28N 02 12.16W
TYPE	Steamship (built 1906)
TONNAGE	3,806

CARGO	Coal and coke
LENGTH	346ft
BEAM	50ft
DRAUGHT	25ft
DATE SUNK	1916
SEA DEPTH	60m

The Finn was attacked and torpedoed by the German submarine U 26. Wreck is upside down and positively identified by the bell which was recovered in 1998. The bell was found by a lucky diver, lying near the end of the mast on the sea bed.

FLUENT

GPS	50 26.40N 01 48.15W
TYPE	Steamship
TONNAGE	3,660
CARGO	Steel ingots and artillery shells
LENGTH	350ft
BEAM	50ft
DATE SUNK	1917.20.07
SEA DEPTH	40m

The identity has not been confirmed for this vessel. The Fluent was on passage from New York to London when attacked by German submarine U-65. The ship was carrying a cargo of steel and oats. She lies upside down on a stony seabed. The ship was sunk 16 miles south of Anvil Point. Local experts think that this could be the wreck of the Saxmundham, a 2,537 British registered steamship, which sank in 1888.

FORESTER

GPS	50 34.36N 02 24.63W
TYPE	Coaster
TONNAGE	191
CARGO	Ballast
LENGTH	97ft
BEAM	22ft

DRAUGHT	9ft
DATE SUNK	1930.12.01
SEA DEPTH	10m

The wreck of the Forester lies parallel to the breakwater to Portland Harbour. The vessel broke free during a storm and drifted through the anchored Royal Naval Atlantic Fleet. The ship eventually struck the breakwater and the crew of six and one stowaway scrambled to safety just before the ship sank.

FRANCISKA

GPS	50 28.18N 02 27.64W
TYPE	Steamship (German)
TONNAGE	669
CARGO	Coal
LENGTH	205ft
BEAM	26ft
DRAUGHT	20ft
DATE SUNK	1889.24.02
SEA DEPTH	48m

The Franciska sank after a collision with the barque, Hono, while on passage from Cardiff to Flushing. The wreck was identified with the recovery of the bell. The ship lies upright and has the remains of a two-cylinder engine. The deck is mostly missing and the wreck stands up to 4metres above the seabed.

FRIGGA

GPS	50 13.602N 02 17.017W
TYPE	Steamship
TONNAGE	1,046
CARGO	Coal 1435 tons
LENGTH	226ft
BEAM	32ft
DRAUGHT	13ft

DATE SUNK	1917.25.08
SEA DEPTH	60m

The Frigga (built in 1900) was torpedoed. The crew of 16 survived the attack, and the position was given at the time of sinking. The wreck has been found and identified with the recovery of the bell. The ship lies upright and is broken up.

FROGNER

GPS	50 31.81N 02 33.44W
TYPE	Steamship (Norwegian)
TONNAGE	1,476
CARGO	Ballast
LENGTH	260ft
BEAM	37ft
DRAUGHT	17ft
DATE SUNK	1918.29.04
SEA DEPTH	35m

Torpedoed by German submarine U-boat 17. The wreck has been positively identified, and has been extensively salvaged. It is very broken up.

GALICIA

GPS	50 33.289N 03 26.393W
TYPE	Steamship (armed)
TONNAGE	5,922
CARGO	Cement and cloth
LENGTH	400ft
BEAM	50ft
DATE SUNK	1917.12.05
SEA DEPTH	17m

The Galicia sank after striking a sea mine. The wreck has been extensively salvaged and is now very broken up. The wreck site covers an area of about two football fields. There is a lot of silt and visibility can be a problem. Among the debris of this wreck can be found old tool kits often covered by the silt. Near the site are growths of local coral. The highest part of the wreck is 14 metres off the seabed. Also among the debris are barrels of solid cement and a large mast lies to one side.

The Galicia is typical of the many First World War wrecks off the coast of Dorset and Devon. She was an armed merchantman of 5,922 tons. On the 12th of May 1917 she struck a sea mine and started to sink, 3 miles east of Teignmouth. The Galicia was in ballast though on board were 59 passengers and crew, who were rescued by the Teignmouth lifeboat, a tug and a naval auxiliary vessel. The vessel is still visible on the sea bed, though broken up.

GALIA

GPS	50 26.41N 01 48.10W
TYPE	Collier
TONNAGE	2,728
CARGO	Coal 3029 tons
LENGTH	300ft
BEAM	39ft
DRAUGHT	20ft
DATE SUNK	1917.24.10
SEA DEPTH	37m

The wreck lies north south and is well broken up. In the area of the midships is one of the boilers. The wreck rises up to 7 metres off the seabed. The Galia was torpedoed by the German submarine UB-40. She lies about 14 miles off Bournemouth on the east Dorset coast.

GARM

GPS	50 16.58N 03 28.44W
TYPE	Steamship (Norwegian)
TONNAGE	725
CARGO	Coal 880 tons
LENGTH	56.63m
BEAM	8.53m
DRAUGHT	3.81m

DATE SUNK	1917.26.08
SEA DEPTH	55m

The Garm was torpedoed while en route from Liverpool to Rouen. Wreck lies upright NE-SW. The vessel lies on her starboard side. A pottery jug was recovered bearing the legend K.A.N. The wreck has not been identified.

GEFFIEN (also known as Gefion)

GPS	50 30.10N 03 15.29W
TYPE	Steamship (Norwegian)
TONNAGE	1,123
CARGO	Coal 1,600 tons
LENGTH	226ft
BEAM	37ft
DRAUGHT	16ft
DATE SUNK	1917.25.10
SEA DEPTH	32m

The Geffien was torpedoed and sunk by the German submarine U-40 The Geffien was on passage from Penarth (S.Wales) to Rouen (N.France). The ship is broken up, with the forward section lying on the starboard side. This is not a popular local dive. The wreck is dark with lots of nets attached the rusting hulk.

GERTRUDE

GPS	50 32.80N 02 27.10W	
TYPE	Steamship	
TONNAGE	1,377	
CARGO	Iron ore	
LENGTH	74.37m	
BEAM	9.81m	
DRAUGHT	5.61m	
DATE SUNK	1894.18.11	
SEA DEPTH	14m	

The Gertrude was driven ashore during a storm. The wreck is very broken up and the boiler lies to the starboard side of the wreck. The vessel's anchor can be seen on the port side.

GIBEL HAMAM

GPS	50 35.86N 02 53.06W
TYPE	Steamship
TONNAGE	647
CARGO	Coal
LENGTH	180ft
BEAM	29ft
DRAUGHT	11ft
DATE SUNK	1918.14.09
SEA DEPTH	33m

The Gibel Hamam was torpedoed by German submarine U-103 and sunk off Abbotsbury. The wreck is broken in two parts down the mid-ships. The hull is structurally failing due to corrosion. The wreck is also known as the Bamburgh, which was the name on the ship's bell.

GLENMORE

GPS	50 35.17N 02 04.90W
TYPE	Tug (Salvage Drifter)
TONNAGE	65
CARGO	Jute and diving equipment
DATE SUNK	1922.24.03
SEA DEPTH	9m

This Weymouth-based tug sank while attempting to salvage a ship, the Treveall, which had gone aground on Kimmeridge Ledges, off the Purbeck coast. The tug holed itself on the wreck and sank.

GLOCLIFFE (known locally as IREX)

GPS	50 27.133N 03 17.407W
TYPE	Steamship
TONNAGE	2,211

CARGO	Coal 3,300 tons
LENGTH	287ft
BEAM	44ft
DRAUGHT	19ft
DATE SUNK	1917.19.08
SEA DEPTH	38m

The ship was torpedoed the German submarine U-40, which killed two of the crew. The wreck is largely intact and lies on the port side. There is a gun on the port side stern section. The wreck is sometimes confused with the nearby wreck of a trawler, the Irex, which lies close by to the Glocliffe. The bell of the Glocliffe was recovered in 1999 by a group of divers out with Diver Down of Babbacombe, Torquay.

GORIZIA (ex Glenmount)

GPS	50 25.80N 02 47.42W
TYPE	Steamship
TONNAGE	1957
CARGO	Steel and brass
LENGTH	249ft
BEAM	43ft
DRAUGHT	21ft
DATE SUNK	1917.30.04
SEA DEPTH	52m

The steamship Gorizia was attacked by a German U-boat, while on passage from New York to Le Havre. The Gorizia was boarded and sunk with scuttling charges. The wreck has been extensively salvaged and is partially dispersed, though there remains a quantity of steel and brass. The brass cargo is in the form of 6-inch die discs, which are a half-inch thick.

GRANE

GPS	50 29.38N 02 42.76W
TYPE	Steamship (Norwegian)
TONNAGE	1,122
CARGO	Coal 1,430 tons

LENGTH	231ft
BEAM	30ft
DRAUGHT	14ft
DATE SUNK	1918
SEA DEPTH	43m

The Grane was on passage to Swansea when she was torpedoed by the German submarine U-80. The bell was recovered in 1986. The wreck is very broken up.

GRELEEN

GPS	50 27.66N 03 13.87W
TYPE	Steamship
TONNAGE	2,286
CARGO	Iron ore
LENGTH	313ft
BEAM	38ft
DRAUGHT	22ft
DATE SUNK	1917.22.09
SEA DEPTH	40m

The Greleen was built in 1894, by Harland and Wolf, of Belfast. The ship was torpedoed by the German submarine U-40. The attack resulted in the death of 19 of the crew. The bell has been recovered and the vessel is badly corroded and broken up.

According to local divers, this is not a popular dive; the hulk is tangled with old fishing nets and there is little of the structure of this vessel to see.

GRETA C (EASTERN TRADER)

GPS	50 21.02N 02 59.12W
TYPE	Freighter
TONNAGE	474
CARGO	Granite chips
LENGTH	170ft
BEAM	24ft

DRAUGHT	9ft
DATE SUNK	1974.07.09
SEA DEPTH	51m

The ship sank in heavy seas, during which the deck hatches collapsed. One member of the crew was drowned. The wreck is 15 miles SW of Portland Bill. The wreck has been positively identified by Lyme Bay Deep Divers. She lies on her starboard side and is largely intact. The Greta is a rare modern wreck. The bell has been recovered from this vessel.

GRIPFAST

GPS	50 25.43N 02 29.95W
TYPE	Steamship
TONNAGE	448
CARGO	Coal 1,272 tons
LENGTH	161ft
BEAM	27ft
DRAUGHT	14ft
DATE SUNK	1940.17.10
SEA DEPTH	46m

The Gripfast sank after being bombed by the Luftwaffe. The wreck was once thought to be that of the Kingston Cairngorm and the wreck has not been positively identified. The Gripfast was carrying 5 survivors from the Rosten after escaping a German E-Boat attack on a convoy in the early years of WW2.

HALSEWELL

GPS	50 34.10N 02 01.75W
TYPE	Sailing (East Indiaman)
TONNAGE	776
CARGO	General cargo, and some silver and gold
DATE SUNK	1786.06.
SEA DEPTH	10m

The Halsewell foundered on rocks between Seacombe and Winspitt with the loss of 166 passengers and crew. There is now very little visible evidence of this wreck. The site was extensively dived in the 1960s and many of the finds can be seen at the museum in Dorchester. The debris of the wreck is hidden by shingle, which covers the bedrock and it is still possible to find coins, copper, brass and cannonballs if one has the patience. The site can be dived at any state of the tide. There is an excellent account of the wreck by Steve Shovlar in his book, Dorset Shipwrecks.

HAROLD'S WRECK see RADASS

HARTBURN

GPS	50 30.74N 02 06.42W
TYPE	Steamship
TONNAGE	2,367
CARGO	Railway-tracks.
LENGTH	303ft
BEAM	43ft
DRAUGHT	20ft
DATE SUNK	1917.15.10
SEA DEPTH	39m

The Hartburn was torpedoed. The stern is extensively damaged. This wreck has not been positively identified and could be the of the Saxmundham.

HARTLEPOOL

GPS	50 36.47N 02 25.96W
TYPE	Steamship
TONNAGE	5,500
CARGO	Ammunition found on wreck
LENGTH	426ft
BEAM	56ft
DRAUGHT	26ft
DATE SUNK	1940.05.07
SEA DEPTH	12m

The Hartlepool was sunk by torpedo by German E-Boats. The bow was salvaged but the rest of the vessel remains on the sea bed and is broken up. The remains are a half mile SE of Weymouth Harbour.

Haytion sunk Portland Harbour

HAYTION (HAM)

GPS	50 34.68N 02 27.52W
TYPE	Steamship
DATE SUNK	1940
SEA DEPTH	3m

The wreck lies in Portland Harbour and is very broken up. Little remains except for the ribs and some old beams. The bottom is silt and there is a danger from sail-boarders above.

HEROINE

GPS	50 40.52N 02 56.13W
TYPE	Sailing barque
TONNAGE	307
CARGO	General cargo
DATE SUNK	1852.26.12
SEA DEPTH	25m

The ship sunk during a gale. The crew and the passengers were rescued and landed at Lyme Regis. The barque was en route from London to Port Phillip (Australia). The ship was extensively salvaged in 1853 and rediscovered and salvaged in 1994 by local dive boat operator, John Walker. The present lifeboat station at Lyme Regis has some recovered bricks from the stricken vessel built into the wall. If you would like to visit the site contact John Walker on 01297 552160, and for more details see the web site at: www.divernet.com/wrecks/heroi596.htm

HILDEGARDE

GPS	50 35.30N 02 06.10W
TYPE	Steamship
TONNAGE	1,886
CARGO	Iron ore 2, 650tons
LENGTH	262ft
DATE SUNK	1900
SEA DEPTH	7m

The Hildegarde ran aground onto the ledges off Kimmeridge and eventually broke up and sank a half-mile south of Freshwater Ledge. The wreck was extensively salvaged and the remains are broken up and dispersed among the ledges and kelp beds of the area. The Hildegarde had been en route from Spain (Almeria) to Newcastle.

HIMALAYA

GPS	50 34.70N 02 26.59W
TYPE	Coal hulk
TONNAGE	3,438
CARGO	Coal
LENGTH	113.66m
BEAM	14.08m
DRAUGHT	10.64m
DATE SUNK	1941.12.06
SEA DEPTH	11m

The vessel had once been a troop ship and conveyed troops to the battles of the Crimean War. The ship was eventually decommissioned and became a coal hulk in Portland Harbour. Portland was the main naval base for the Channel fleet. The Himalaya was sunk during one of the many attacks launched on the naval base by the Luftwaffe during the spring of 1941.

When it was launched, the three masted troop ship was the world's largest vessel.

HMS A3

GPS	50 31.41N 02 11.25W
TYPE	Submarine
TONNAGE	190
LENGTH	105ft
DATE SUNK	1912.02.02
SEA DEPTH	38m

The naval submarine HMS A3 collided with HMS Hazard. The collision left a large hole in the hull of the submarine. The submarine sank immediately and all 13 crew were drowned. The submarine was eventually located and raised and towed back to Portsmouth where the dead were removed from the hull. After the naval inquiry into the tragedy, the hulk was towed out to sea and sunk. The large battleship HMS St Vincent sank the A3 with gunfire south of Worbarrow Tout. The submarine lies upright with a slight list. The conning tower is still intact, but the hatch is missing.

HMS AMAZON

GPS	CLASSIFIED
TYPE	Screw powered sloop (built 1865)
TONNAGE	1081
LENGTH	187ft
BEAM	36ft
DRAUGHT	9ft
DATE SUNK	1866.10.07
SEA DEPTH	60m

The ship was located and identified by divers on the Weymouth-based boats, Wey Chieftain II and Skin Deep. The position is not shown due to the historic nature of this wreck. Interested parties should contact either of the above boats, which are based in Weymouth. The vessel lies upright and is intact but broken down to 3m off the seabed. The Amazon sank after colliding with SS Osprey. Lyme Bay Deep Divers made the identification. There is to be an archaeological investigation of this site.

HMS ARFON

GPS	50 28.18N 02 10.37W
TYPE	Trawler (minesweeper, armed)
TONNAGE	227 displacement
DATE SUNK	1917.30.04
SEA DEPTH	40m

This armed trawler sank when it hit a mine. The wreck was discovered in 1998 and is 7 miles south of Warbarrow Bay. The trawler lies upright but is very broken up.

HMS BITTERN

GPS	50 18.13N 02.59W
TYPE	Warship (Destroyer)
TONNAGE	360 displacement
LENGTH	210ft
DATE SUNK	1918.04.04
SEA DEPTH	60m

HMS Bittern sank after a collision. The destroyer lies in two parts and was positively identified by Lyme Bay Deep Divers in 1999.

HMS BLACKWOOD

GPS	50 12 20N 02 14 60W
TYPE	Warship (Frigate)
TONNAGE	1,150 displacement
LENGTH	300ft
BEAM	35ft

DATE SUNK	1944.15.06
SEA DEPTH	60m

The frigate was torpedoed and the bows were blown off by the German submarine U-boat 764. There was an attempted salvage, but the ship sank while under tow. After the war she was used in anti-submarine exercises and regularly depth charged. The wreck is very smashed up.

HMS BOADICEA

GPS	50 25.66N 02 45.92W
TYPE	Warship (Destroyer)
TONNAGE	1,360 displacement
LENGTH	323ft
BEAM	32ft
DRAUGHT	12ft
DATE SUNK	1944.13.06
SEA DEPTH	50m

HMS Boadicea sunk after an attack by the Luftwaffe towards the end of WW2. The forward section was destroyed in the attack. The ship is a war grave and contains the remains of 175 crew, who perished as a result of the attack. The bell was recovered for identification of this wreck. The stern section is upright and intact with four 4.7-inch guns. There are depth charges in the racks and torpedoes in the tubes. The bow and bridge section are demolished.

HMS BUCCANEER

GPS	50 29.36N 02 41.77W
TYPE	Tug
TONNAGE	840
LENGTH	165ft
BEAM	32ft
DRAUGHT	11ft
DATE SUNK	1946.26.08
SEA DEPTH	43m

The Royal Naval tug HMS Buccaneer was sunk while towing a target, a hazard of this dangerous occupation. The wreck lies on its port side and still has its gun (4.7inch) and twin screws.

HMS CLYDE

GPS	50 32.06N 02 56.36W
TYPE	Trawler (Patrol Mine Sweeper)
TONNAGE	146
LENGTH	97ft
BEAM	20.6ft
DRAUGHT	11ft
DATE SUNK	1917.14.10
SEA DEPTH	40m

HMS Clyde was a requisitioned trawler. The wreck lies upright and is well preserved, although the wheelhouse is now missing. There is a large dent to the rear on the vessel on the transom.

HMS DELIGHT

GPS	50 15.05N 02 42.58W
TYPE	DESTROYER (built 1932)
TONNAGE	1,375 dis
LENGTH	96.93m
BEAM	10.06m
DATE SUNK	1940.29.07
SEA DEPTH	60m

The destroyer was bombed by the Luftwaffe and quickly sank, breaking into three sections. The centre section is upside down. The stern has two propellers to the side. During the attack the destroyer caught fire which caused a large explosion. Six naval crew perished in the action.

HMS EMPRESS OF INDIA

GPS	50 29.758N 02 57.937W
TYPE	Warship (Battleship)
TONNAGE	15,585

LENGTH	380ft
BEAM	75ft
DRAUGHT	27ft
DATE SUNK	1913.04.11
SEA DEPTH	48m

The Empress of India was used as a gunnery target. The wreck lies upside down and there has been some salvage. The bows are to the east and the foremast protrudes from the north side of the wreck. The wreck is a popular site with local divers and is described as one of the best wrecks in the bay. There are still plenty of portholes on the wreck and the rusting hulk attracts a large amount of fish life.

HMS FORMIDABLE

GPS	50 13.12N 02 03.59W
TYPE	Warship (Battleship)
TONNAGE	15,000 (Displacement)
LENGTH	430ft
BEAM	75ft
DRAUGHT	29ft
DATE SUNK	1915.01.01
SEA DEPTH	60m

The battleship was torpedoed while on exercise with the 5th Battle Squadron. Over 540 officers and ratings were lost. The wreck lies upside down, with the hull mostly intact except for a split in the front of the bridge. The props are also missing. This vessel is a war grave and should be treated with respect.

The sinking of the Formidable was a disaster for the Royal Navy and a tragic loss of life. Admiral Bayly was the new commander of the Fifth Battle Squadron, having transferred from the Northern Fleet. Shortly before Christmas he received permission to take the squadron from Nore (in Essex) to Portland, off which he was to train and exercise. He sailed down the Channel with an escort of 6 destroyers, which returned to Nore after reaching Folkstone. For the remaining journey, to Portland, there was to be no protective screen, apart from the light cruisers HMS Topaz and HMS Diamond. The Admiral arrived off Portland with his squadron at daybreak, on the 31st of December. The training and firing exercise in Lyme Bay lasted all day. At dusk, the Admiral decided against putting into Portland Harbour, and remained at sea, to restart the exercise in the morning. (There had been no reported German submarine activity in the area) The squadron proceeded to sail east towards the Isle of Wight. Shortly after dark the course was changed to west (this was in accordance with naval regulations, to forestall attack by Submarine). The night was clear, with good visibility and a bright moon. The ships kept a straight course, the two light cruisers to the front and the Formidable to the rear. Unknown to Admiral Bayly, all the previous afternoon, a German submarine had observed the exercise and had stalked the squadron, waiting for a chance to attack the battleship. Even the abrupt change of course, at dusk was pointless, with the moon silhouetting the outline of the vast warship. At 2.30 a.m., as the squadron drew near to Start Point, off the Devon coast, the German submarine

fired its torpedo, striking the Formidable, in the starboard side and knocking out the engine, the ship soon listed twenty degrees. There was no panic after the initial attack, although the weather was deteriorating. The position of the ship was hopeless, as she foundered in the swell, disabled with no steerage. It was decided to start evacuating the ship. The ships pinnace, launch and two boats were filled with sailors. One of the boats capsized, in the swell. The light cruiser, HMS Topaz came alongside and succeeded in taking off 43 men, in difficult conditions. An hour passed, when a second torpedo struck the Formidable, this time on the portside. The ship swung up onto an even keel, as the sea rushed into the gaping hole. Water logged, with no engine power the crew were unable to launch the rest of the lifeboats. HMS Topaz tried to fetch a passing liner, but with no success. HMS Diamond (the other light cruiser) was ordered to standoff from the Formidable, due to the danger of another torpedo attack. The order was given to abandon ship at 4.45am, two and a half hours after the first torpedo had struck the dreadnought. As the sea and the wind rose the crew scrambled over the side, into the freezing January water. The ship went down, bow first, her screws and rudder standing clear of the water, she sank quickly. The Brixam trawler 'Provident' picked up the Formidable's launch! The launch was overcrowded and nearly sinking. The Provident was able to come alongside and took off 71 sailors. The gale and storm rapidly dispersed the surviving flotilla of lifeboats. One lifeboat was found the next day, on the beach at Abbotsbury, empty and upside down. A second overcrowded lifeboat managed to avoid sinking in the storm and ended up on the town beach at Lyme Regis. The lifeboat contained the dead and the barely living that had endured freezing temperatures and near capsize during the storm. The survivors and bodies were taken into the nearby by pub the Pilot Boat, where a temporary morgue was established in the beer cellar. One sailor though to be dead was revived by the licking of the landlord's dog, Lassie. The story of the dog reviving the man was reported in newspapers around the world as the only bit of good news to come from this disaster. The story was the inspiration for the Hollywood film of Lassie.

Out of a total crew of 780 crew only 233 survived. At the subsequent inquiry Admiral Bayly was relieved of his command.

HMS FISGARD 11

GPS	50 28.25N 02 29.51W
TYPE	Warship (Naval training ship)
TONNAGE	6,010 displacement
LENGTH	280ft
BEAM	54ft
DRAUGHT	23ft

DATE SUNK   1914.17.09

SEA DEPTH   68m

HMS Fisgard was the former battleship HMS Invincible. It was later
decommissioned and renamed the Fisgard and became a fleet training ship
for the Royal Navy. The ship sank while under tow with the loss of 21 crew.
The wreck lies in a deep depression off Portland Bill and stands up to 13
metres off the seabed. The stumps of the masts lie to the side, and the
original teak framework has now perished. The propellers are also missing.
The warship lies upside down and against a ledge.

HMS HARSTADT

GPS	50 24.11N 03 01.19W
TYPE	Whaler -minesweeper
TONNAGE	258ft
LENGTH	119ft
BEAM	24ft
DRAUGHT	14ft
DATE SUNK	1943.27.02
SEA DEPTH	56m

HMS Harstadt was a requisitioned Norwegian whaler, used for
minesweeping during the Second World War. She was attacked and sunk
by German motor gunboats operating from Cherbourg, while on convoy
duty.

The stern of the Harstadt lies upright and is intact. The bow is located to the
starboard side and to the NE. An acoustic hammer frame is on the bows
and the hammer is on the seabed. A 37mm gun bandstand is also to be
found to the side of the wreck on the seabed. The wreck has been
positively identified by Lyme Bay Deep Divers The Harstadt lies close to the
wreck of the MV Modavia both were part of the convoy WP300.

HMS HICKORY

GPS	50 29.43N 02 54.61W
TYPE	Trawler (minesweeper)
TONNAGE	530
LENGTH	150ft

BEAM   28ft

DATE SUNK   1940.22.10

SEA DEPTH   43m

The requisitioned trawler struck a mine and sank with the loss of 25 crew.

HMS HOOD - scuttled as a block ship to Portland

HMS HOOD

GPS   50 34.14N 02 25.31W

TYPE   Battleship

TONNAGE   14,150 displacement

LENGTH   380ft

BEAM   75ft

DATE SUNK   1914 04.11

SEA DEPTH   15m

HMS Hood, a Royal Sovereign class battleship, was sunk as a block ship at the start of WW1. There were concerns about a German submarine attack on the naval base at Portland and it was decided to seal off the southern approach to the harbour. The Hood was scuttled and inverted on sinking. She lays 2metres below the surface, at low water. For those wishing to dive the Hood always check the tides as there is a strong current in this area of the harbour. Much of the wreck is now in a fragile state, though there is plenty of marine life in the area

HMS L.24

GPS	50 22.53N 02 37.91W
TYPE	Submarine
TONNAGE	1080
LENGTH	239ft
BEAM	24ft
DRAUGHT	28ft
DATE SUNK	1924.10.01
SEA DEPTH	55m

The L.24 submarine sank after a collision with HMS Resolution. All 36 crew drowned in the accident. The hatches of the submarine are open. Near to this wreck is a newly discovered vessel, the Marie Theresa. Little is known of this wreck apart from the name on the bell, which was found.

HMS LANDRAIL

GPS	50 33.75N 02 37.54W
TYPE	Curlew Class Gun Boat
TONNAGE	790
LENGTH	195ft
BEAM	28ft
DATE SUNK	1906.04.10
SEA DEPTH	31m

HMS Landrail was pre-WW1 torpedo-gunboat. The wreck is often confused with that of with that of HMS Hazard. HMS Landrail was sunk while under tow after being used for target practice. The hull had been filled with cork, which proved insufficient. The wreck lies in two parts.

HMS LORD HAILSHAM

GPS	50 23.25N 03 02.84W
TYPE	Trawler (Anti submarine)
TONNAGE	445
LENGTH	156ft
BEAM	26ft

DATE SUNK   1943.27.02

SEA DEPTH   50m

The Hailsham was attacked and sunk by E-Boats while on convoy duty (WP300). The wreck has been identified by Lyme Bay Deep Divers. She lies on the starboard side with the bows to the south. Ordnance on the wreck includes numerous rounds of 20mm shell and depth charges. A popular dive with local clubs.

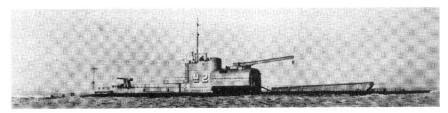

The M2- the open hangar doors can be seen on the bow

HMS M2

GPS	50 34.60N 02 34.01W
TYPE	Submarine
TONNAGE	1,650
LENGTH	296ft
BEAM	25ft
DATE SUNK	1932.26.01
SEA DEPTH	31m

The M2 was lost with all hands, after sinking rapidly. The submarine was unusual in design and had a hanger door to the front of the deck for launching a seaplane. The inquiry into the sinking blamed the faulty closing of the doors. While researching this book I came into contact with an elderly mariner who had been on this vessel. He stated that: the vessel had a tendency to kick back into the water when first breaking the surface. There would also be a competition to see how fast the crew could open the doors. Given the swell off the Chesil Beach it would seem a large volume of water rushed from the stern when the vessel surfaced and poured into the recently opened hanger doors. The vessel sank with all hands and is a designated war grave. The outer hull is now rotting and the props are missing. It is an interesting and recommended dive.

HMS P.555

GPS	50 30.96N 02 33.43W
TYPE	Submarine S Class
TONNAGE	1,062
LENGTH	219ft
BEAM	21ft
DRAUGHT	16ft
DATE SUNK	1947.25.08
SEA DEPTH	34m

The P.555 was an American built submarine, which was given to the Royal Navy for use in Second World War. At the end of the war the submarine was decommissioned and scuttled and then used as a target for the early development and testing of sonar acoustic direction finding equipment. The wreck is in good condition.

HMS RECOIL (ex Blankenburg)

GPS	50 26.41N 02 44.11W
TYPE	Trawler
TONNAGE	344
DATE SUNK	1940.28.09
SEA DEPTH	48m

The identity of this vessel is not positive. The requisitioned trawler was sunk while on anti-submarine operations. The wreck lies upright and is in two parts and contains ordnance, which includes live depth charges.

HMS REMINDO

GPS	50 26.16N 02 43.74W
TYPE	Trawler (Anti submarine)
TONNAGE	256
LENGTH	117ft
BEAM	27ft
DATE SUNK	1918.02.02
SEA DEPTH	50m

The cause of the sinking of HMS Remindo is not known and the wreck has not been positively identified, though it is probably the trawler. The wreck lies upright and is broken in parts. There are live 303 rounds. A distinguishing feature of the wreck is the triple expansion engine.

HMS SAFARI

GPS	50 25.34N 02 02.54W
TYPE	Submarine. S-class group 3
TONNAGE	715
LENGTH	61.72m
BEAM	7.32m
DATE SUNK	1946.08.01
SEA DEPTH	40m

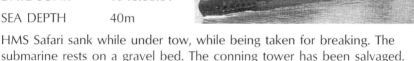

HMS Safari sank while under tow, while being taken for breaking. The submarine rests on a gravel bed. The conning tower has been salvaged.

HMS SARGASSO

GPS	50 31.53N 01 42.20W
TYPE	Minesweeper
TONNAGE	228
DATE SUNK	1943.06.06
SEA DEPTH	35m

The minesweeper sank after hitting a mine, and lies upside down, with the bows pointing due west.

HMS SIDON

GPS	50 32.96N 02 38.49W
TYPE	Submarine. S class group
TONNAGE	990
LENGTH	217ft
BEAM	24ft
DATE SUNK	1957.14.06
SEA DEPTH	36m

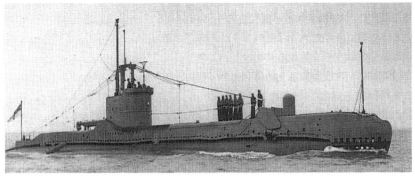

HMS Sidon was severely damaged in Portland Harbour when an unstable torpedo exploded (powered by Hydrogen sulphide). As a result of the accident the Royal Navy abandoned this type of torpedo design. (The same unstable fuel element is thought to be the cause of the sinking of the Russian nuclear submarine, the Kursk that sank in 2000). The Sidon was severely damaged by the accident and beyond salvage. The submarine was later towed out to sea and sunk as a sonar target. The Sidon has recently been bought by Deep Quest Ltd, as a test facility, for new salvage techniques.

HMS WARRIOR II

GPS	50 21.56N 02 12.23W
TYPE	Motor yacht
TONNAGE	1,124
LENGTH	284ft
BEAM	32ft
DRAUGHT	17ft
DATE SUNK	1940.11.07
SEA DEPTH	54m

HMS Warrior II was a requisitioned luxury yacht, built in 1904. She was later bombed and sunk by the Luftwaffe off Portland Bill.

HOPEDALE

GPS	
TYPE	Steamship
TONNAGE	1,746
CARGO	Coal
LENGTH	280ft
BEAM	38ft
DRAUGHT	18ft
DATE SUNK	1908.24.07
SEA DEPTH	35m

The Hopedale ran into fog banks and collided with the SS Elmsgarth. She sank in 35m of water just off St Catherine's Point.

ILLINIOS

GPS	49 58.50N 02 19.97W
TYPE	Tanker
TONNAGE	5,225
CARGO	Ballast
DATE SUNK	1917.18.03
SEA DEPTH	68m

The position of the Illinios is 40 miles south of Portland Bill. The bell has been recovered. The wreck lies upright and is intact and is one of the best-preserved wrecks off the Dorset coast. The deck is at 58 metres. If you wish to dive this vessel, contact the local dive boats that operate out of Weymouth such as Skin Deep or Wey Chieftain II.

INNISINVER

GPS	50 29.40N 02 35.22W
TYPE	Motor vessel
TONNAGE	126
CARGO	China clay
LENGTH	74ft
BEAM	18.7ft

DRAUGHT   8.8ft

DATE SUNK   1930.09.09

SEA DEPTH   42m

The Innisinver sank after hitting a submerged object. The wreck is fairly intact and complete.

IOLANTHE

GPS   50 27.64N 02 07.96W

TYPE   Steamship

TONNAGE   3,081

CARGO   Military stores, railway trucks.

LENGTH   325ft

BEAM   49ft

DATE SUNK   1917.25.12

SEA DEPTH   45m

Iolanthe. A cargo of railway trucks

The Iolanthe was torpedoed and sunk by a German submarine U-75, while trying to reach Portland harbour. The wreck is broken up but she still has her cargo of railway trucks.

ISBJORN

GPS	50 22.40N 03 03.56W
TYPE	Steamship
TONNAGE	597
CARGO	Coal
LENGTH	169ft
BEAM	27ft
DRAUGHT	14ft
DATE SUNK	1944.17.12
SEA DEPTH	56m

The identity of the wreck has been confirmed by Lyme Bay Deep Divers. The vessel lies upright with little sign of damage. The wreck is largely intact and recommended by local divers as a site worth visiting. The bell has been recovered.

JAMES FENNEL

GPS	50 32.78N 02 27.51W
TYPE	Trawler
TONNAGE	215
LENGTH	123ft
BEAM	22ft
DATE SUNK	1920.16.01
SEA DEPTH	18m

The ship steered onto the rocks during thick fog and was holed. There was an attempt at salvage, which failed. All the crew were saved. The wreck lies at 15 metres and is now very broken up and scattered over the sandy and rocky area. It is best dived when the wind is in an easterly direction. The wreck is 80 metres off shore opposite a window-like hole in the face of the cliffs to the north of Blacknor Point. The stern is complete and there are parts of the engine and boiler to be seen.

KENDAL CASTLE

GPS	50 21.38N 03 24.37W
TYPE	Steamship
TONNAGE	3,885
CARGO	Ballast
LENGTH	350ft
BEAM	50ft
DRAUGHT	26ft
DATE SUNK	1918.15.09
SEA DEPTH	

The Kendal Castle was torpedoed killing all crew. There is a 2 metres scour on the west side of the ship. The vessel lies upright and the bow is broken open. There are also lots of old fishing nets on this wreck. In the vicinity of this vessel are three other wrecks. They are the Dudley Rose, the Bleamore and the Beustan. The Kendal Castle was part of the James Chambers Line. Pottery has been recovered from it, which provided the identity of the wreck.

KONSHAUG (ex Scilia)

GPS	50 19.61N 03 00.15W
TYPE	STEAMSHIP (built 1898)
TONNAGE	1,156
CARGO	1,250 tons patent fuel blocks
LENGTH	217ft
BEAM	32ft
DRAUGHT	21ft
DATE SUNK	1942.09.07
SEA DEPTH	59m

The ship was torpedoed by E-Boats with other vessels, which were part of the convoy WP183. She lies inverted with the stern to the east. Patent coal fuel blocks litter the seabed. There is a hole near the keel mid-ships. The ship was located and positively identified by Lyme Bay Deep Divers. The ship sank 30 seconds after the attack. There is another wreck close by called the Phoenix.

KYARRA

GPS	50 34.91N 01 56.57W
TYPE	Steamship
TONNAGE	6,953
LENGTH	415ft
BEAM	52ft
DRAUGHT	28ft
DATES SUNK	1918.06.05
SEA DEPTH	34m

The vessel was being used as a hospital ship when it was torpedoed off Durlston Head. The ship is now owned by Kingston BSAC who should be notified if anything is removed from the site. The wreck is one of the most popular to dive on this area of the Dorset coast.

The engines of the Kyarra at the shipyard on the Clyde
before their installation in the ship

L.H.CARL

GPS	50 23.98N 02 46.46W
TYPE	Steamship
TONNAGE	1,916
CARGO	Coal
LENGTH	280ft
BEAM	40ft
DRAUGHT	18ft

| DATE SUNK | 1917.20.07 |
| SEA DEPTH | 54m 45m to the top |

A large wreck with a spectacular stern section, which rises 10 metres off the seabed. Brass identification letters were taken from the front of the bridge.

L24 (built 1919)

GPS	50 22.50N 02 37.79W
TYPE	submarine. built 1920
TONNAGE	1,080
LENGTH	239ft
BEAM	24ft
DRAUGHT	14ft
DATE SUNK	1924.10.01
SEA DEPTH	54ft

Sunk in collision with the battleship HMS Resolution, with a loss of 36 crew. The conning tower rises up 6 metres from the seabed. The wreck is intact.

LANDING CRAFT

| GPS | 50 34.51N 02 28.20W |
| TYPE | Landing craft |

LANDING CRAFT

GPS	50 34.99N 02 25.59W
TYPE	Landing craft
SEA DEPTH	15m

A small intact landing craft about a half-mile due west of the eastern boat channel.

LANDING CRAFT

GPS	50 35.66N 02 20.44W
TYPE	Landing craft
SEA DEPTH	21m

The landing craft is a complete wreck, and the sea bed is very silty and easily disturbed. Little current.

LANDING CRAFT

GPS	50 35.39N 02 20.26W
TYPE	Landing craft
LENGTH	30ft
SEA DEPTH	22m

The craft is intact and lies upright.

LANDING CRAFT

GPS	50 35 58N 02 25 78W
TYPE	Landing craft
SEA DEPTH	15m

There are two landing craft at this site about 7 metres apart.

LANDING CRAFT Portland

GPS	BOOK PG 27
TYPE	Landing craft

LANDING CRAFT Portland Harbour

GPS	BOOK PG 27
TYPE	Landing craft

LANDING CRAFT (Chesil Beach)

GPS	50 34.41N 02 28.22W
TYPE	Landing craft

LANDING CRAFT (Lulworth)

GPS	50 36.93N 02 15.05W
TYPE	Landing craft

LANDING CRAFT LCT

GPS	BOOK PG 84
TYPE	Landing craft

LANDING CRAFT TANK (MARK 3)

GPS	50 23.26N 03 01.24
TYPE	Naval landing craft
LENGTH	192ft
BEAM	31ft
SEA_DEPTH	56m

LENDORA

GPS	677 682 Ordnance Survey map position.
TYPE	Yacht
TONNAGE	15
DATE SUNK	1951.08.09

The Lendora caught a rope around the prop and ran aground off Portland Bill. The wreck site can be snorkelled but beware of the tides further off shore.

LENY (bow)

GPS	50 38.84N 01 52.56W bow
GPS	50 38.80N 01 52.50W stern
TYPE	Coaster (Dutch) MV
TONNAGE	343
CARGO	Coal
LENGTH	136ft
BEAM	24ft
DRAUGHT	10ft
DATE SUNK	1942.23.06
SEA DEPTH	17m

The Dutch coaster struck a sea mine and blew up.

LICENSE TO KILL

GPS	50 34.40N 02 03.83W
TYPE	Sailing
CARGOP	Ballast
LENGTH	32ft
DATE SUNK	1981.25.07

The sloop sank after it caught fire. It is located about 1 mile south of Chapman's Poole, Purbeck.

LORD STEWART

GPS	50 29.612N 03 16.988W
TYPE	Steamship (armed)
TONNAGE	1,445
CARGO	Ballast
LENGTH	248ft
BEAM	36ft
DRAUGHT	16ft
DATE SUNK	1918.16.09
SEA DEPTH	42m

The ship was torpedoed by the German submarine U-104. There is still a small deck gun on the stern of the wreck. The ship lies upright and is broken in two. Divers should beware as phosphorus has been found on this wreck and when exposed to the air will spontaneously combust, along with any diver holding it!

LST 507

GPS	50 27.15N 02 43.55W
TYPE	Landing Ship Tanks (USA)
TONNAGE	1,652
CARGO	Lorries, armaments and ordnance
LENGTH	328ft
BEAM	50ft
DRAUGHT	10ft

DATE SUNK   1944.28.04

SEA DEPTH   48m

The landing craft was part of a convoy practising the D-day landings. The manoeuvres were known as Operation Tiger, which became a major catastrophe when the lightly guarded convoy of assorted landing craft was attacked by an opportunistic patrolling group of German E-Boats operating out of Cherbourg. The craft was one of a number that were attacked and sunk. The vessel went down with 531 American servicemen and all equipment. The true extent of this attack was only known after the war. The wreck lies NE/SW, with the stern N/ENE and is located about 12 miles off Portland Bill. The landing craft is broken into two sections, both rest upside down, the echo sound gives the appearance of two separate wrecks. The stern section is the SE part of the wreck.

A survivor of the attack on Tank Landing ships
docked back at Dartmouth

LST 531

GPS	50 26.05N 02 44.65W
TYPE	Landing Ship Tanks (USA)
TONNAGE	1,652
CARGO	Trucks and amphibious vehicles
LENGTH	326ft
BEAM	50ft
DRAUGHT	10ft
DATE SUNK	1944.28.04
SEA DEPTH	47m

Sunk after an attack by E-boats, with the loss of 434 American soldiers and crew. Like LST 507 it was taking part in Operation Tiger in preparation for the D-Day landings. There is a small boat trapped under the upturned hull. LST 531 lies intact but is upside down with the stern section to NW. Research by Lyme Bay Deep Divers suggests that these identical vessels (LST 507 and LST 531) can be separately identified, by the remains of the LST 531's forward boats, which are still in position. On LST 507, the forward boats were launched during the evacuation of the vessel.

LUCINDA

GPS	50 25.93N 02 48.67W
TYPE	Sailing (Schooner)
TONNAGE	60
CARGO	Mixed metals
LENGTH	79ft
BEAM	16ft
DATE SUNK	1914.30.07
SEA DEPTH	52m

The schooner foundered 14 miles WSW of Portland Bill. Locally the Lucinda is known as the Chain Wreck. Lyme Bay Deep Divers tentatively identified the wreck as the Lucinda in an uncharted position.

MAJORCA

GPS	50 20.20N 02 57.56W
TYPE	Motor vessel (Panamanian)
TONNAGE	439
CARGO	Bagged fertiliser
LENGTH	167ft
BEAM	28ft
DRAUGHT	10ft
DATE SUNK	1982.18.09
SEA DEPTH	45m

The cargo of fertiliser shifted in rough seas while en route from Rotterdam to Teignmouth. The wreck lies upright. The bell was recovered in 1993. Divers should beware as the wreck is covered in fishing nets.

MARGUERITE (Benny's Wreck)

GPS	50 36.13N 02 58.73W
TYPE	Collier (French)
TONNAGE	1,544
CARGO	Ballast
LENGTH	260ft
BEAM	37ft
DRAUGHT	16ft
DATE SUNK	1917.28.06
SEA DEPTH	33m

The ship is also known locally as Benny's Wreck, and is now a twisted pile of metal. Local boats regularly fish the area and there are plenty of fish. The highest point is 7.5m off the seabed. The visibility is usually bad. The engine is on its side, one boiler on end and one horizontal. This is not a favourite wreck with some local divers.

MARIE DES ISLES

GPS	50 28.10N 03 16.72W
TYPE	Trawler (Vivier Crabber)
LENGTH	64ft
BEAM	20ft
DRAUGHT	10ft
DATE SUNK	1980.14.11
SEA DEPTH	36m

The crabber sank while under tow in heavy weather. The wreck is complete with the cabin.

MARIE THERESE

GPS	50 21.31N 02 37.31W
TYPE	Trawler
LENGTH	140ft
SEA DEPTH	56m

This vessel is a mystery. Lyme Bay Deep Divers discovered the Therese, and the bell was recovered, but the identity of the vessel and the name on the bell could not be traced.

MARJOLENE

GPS	50 14.34N 03 09.23W
TYPE	TRAWLER
DATE SUNK	1956.22.12
SEA DEPTH	60m

The trawler is upright and intact.

MARTHA

GPS	50 27.25N 02 38.17W
TYPE	Steamship
TONNAGE	676
CARGO	Coal 800 tons
LENGTH	185ft
BEAM	27ft
DRAUGHT	12ft
DATE SUNK	1918.07.03
SEA DEPTH	46m

The Martha was attacked and sunk by the German submarine U-80. The wreck is fairly intact, and lies NE-SW.

MEAT BOAT (see STRYN)

GPS	50 21.618N 03 11.863W
SEA DEPTH	40m

The Meat Boat is thought to be the wreck of the Stryn, and is 10 miles off Berry Head. The compass stand has been recovered. The vessel is broken in half. There has been no positive identification of this wreck.

MEKNES

GPS	50 11.40N 02 13.80W
TYPE	Hospital ship
TONNAGE	6,127
LENGTH	413ft
BEAM	55ft
DRAUGHT	28ft
DATE SUNK	1940.24.07
SEA DEPTH	60m

The bow lies on her port side and is very smashed up. The ship is upright.

MEMNON (ex Plessey, built 1890)

GPS	50 12.27N 02 40.91W
TYPE	Steamship
TONNAGE	3,203
CARGO	General, 3,300 tons of African products
LENGTH	346ft
BEAM	41ft
DRAUGHT	27ft
DATE SUNK	1917.12.03
SEA DEPTH	60m

An interesting cargo, which included palm oil, groundnuts and peanuts. The ship was torpedoed by the German submarine U-66. Six crew were killed in the attack. Lyme Bay Deep Divers recovered the bell in 1999.

MERCHANT ROYAL (ex Goodwood)

GPS	50 20.08N 02 29.77W
TYPE	Steamship
TONNAGE	5,008
CARGO	Steel and wood
LENGTH	401ft
BEAM	55ft

DRAUGHT	26ft
DATE SUNK	1946.03.07
SEA DEPTH	53m

The Merchant Royal's bell was recovered in 1984. The full name of the ship on the recovered bell is Goodwood. The Merchant Royal sank after a mid-channel collision. The vessel is upright and intact. The bow is due south. The ship has been salvaged though much of this wreck remains intact.

MINERVA

GPS	50 29.61N 02 58.34W
TYPE	Steamship, 3 Masted clipper. Norwegian
TONNAGE	518
LENGTH	182ft
BEAM	25ft
DRAUGHT	15ft
DATE SUNK	1917.10.05
SEA DEPTH	43m

The Minerva was built in 1864 and was an early iron sailing steam vessel that still had the clipper sweeping bow with a flush deck. The Minerva was captured by a German submarine while en route from Caen to Swansea. The vessel was sunk with scuttle charges. There is a single compound engine. The identity of the vessel has been confirmed by Lyme Bay Deep Divers.

MINIOTA (ex Hackness)

GPS	50 03.42N 02 29.15W
TYPE	Steamship (Canadian)
TONNAGE	6,422
CARGO	Silver and 3 tons munitions
LENGTH	128m
DATE SUNK	1917.31.08
SEA DEPTH	65m

The Miniota, the Silver Wreck. The ship lies in mid channel in shipping lanes. The cargo manifest lists silver and munitions. The estimated value of the silver, which has not been found, is over £200,000. The wreck is a difficult dive and was only positively identified in 1999. There are large quantities of munitions on the wreck and large quantity of the mineral, malachite. This wreck probably has more myth and legend about it than any other on the Dorset coast and has already claimed the life of one diver. The Miniota was part of a convoy en route for London from Montreal. The Miniota was to the rear of the convoy when it was attacked by the German submarine U-19. The torpedo tore a large hole in the ship, flooding the engine room.

The wreck has deteriorated over the years and parts of the ship have collapsed; there are large quantities of ordnance on the wreck. The cargo manifest includes 200 tons of brass, 500 tons of TNT, 29 tons of explosives, 1,044 shells, 50 tons of aluminium, along with a large quantity of silver. If you are interested in seeing this wreck contact Grahame Knott on telephone 01305 771371 who is the skipper of Wey Chieftain II.

MODAVIA

GPS	50 24.41N 03 01.91W
TYPE	Motor Vessel (Donaldson)
TONNAGE	4,858
CARGO	Aluminium, zinc, copper
LENGTH	387ft
BEAM	53ft
DRAUGHT	28ft
DATE SUNK	1943.27.02
SEA DEPTH	53m

The ship sank after an attack by E-Boats, while part of a convoy (WP300). She lies on her side and has been extensively damaged in later salvage operations.

MOIDART

GPS	50 34.03N 02 47.29W
TYPE	Steamship (armed)
TONNAGE	1,303
CARGO	Coal and steel
LENGTH	243ft

BEAM	32ft
DRAUGHT	16ft
DATE SUNK	1918.09.06
SEA DEPTH	40m

The ship was torpedoed amidships, and the bow lies upright. The ship was on passage from south Wales to northern France. The Moidart was built 1872. Part of the amidships have collapsed and the wreck stands up to 8 metres above the seabed. A rare 20 cwt gun was salvaged from this vessel. The wreck is about 7 miles SE of Lyme Regis. The stern lies 15 metres to the south of the main wreck site.

MONTANES

GPS	50 34.56N 02 03.35W
TYPE	Cargo ship
TONNAGE	1,045
CARGO	Silver manganese
LENGTH	61.04m
BEAM	9.24m
DRAUGHT	5.24m
DATE SUNK	1906.23.11
SEA DEPTH	6-12m

The general cargo on the Montanes included wine, cork, silver ore and canary seed. The ship struck the rocks and ledges underneath St Albans Head. There is still plenty of debris to seen but beware of the tide especially on the flood.

MYRTLEDENE

GPS	50 32.20N 02 27.30W
TYPE	Steamship (British)
TONNAGE	2,571
CARGO	Iron ore
LENGTH	95.25m
BEAM	12.31m
DRAUGHT	7.50m

DATE SUNK   1912.25.03

SEA DEPTH   10m

The ship was wrecked near Mutton Cove. The remains are in shallow water.

NOR

GPS   OS 665 775 shore dive, off Chesil Beach

TYPE   Sailing (Schooner)

TONNAGE   1,251

CARGO   Salt

LENGTH   70.10m

BEAM   9.69m

DRAUGHT   4.94m

DATE SUNK   1887.18.01

SEA DEPTH   6-12m

The schooner ran aground in fog. The wreck lies about 100 metres south of the wreck of the Royal Adelaide. The wreck is broken up but if the pebbles are cleared away the propeller and shafts can be seen together with parts of the boiler.

NORMANDY

GPS   50 25.00N 01 55.00W

TYPE   Paddle steamer

TONNAGE   550

CARGO   General

LENGTH   210ft

DATE SUNK   1870.03

SEA DEPTH   40m

The Normandy was owned by London and Southwest Railways and built in 1863. She sank after a collision in thick fog while on passage from Southampton to Jersey. AS a result of this accident thirty-seven passengers and crew were lost.

NORTHVILLE

GPS	50 24.45N 03 24.63W
TYPE	Collier
TONNAGE	2,472
CARGO	Coal
LENGTH	304ft
BEAM	44ft
DRAUGHT	21ft
DATE SUNK	1918.17.02
SEA DEPTH	42m

The Northville lies upright and in good preservation. The ship was torpedoed by the German submarine U-33. The wreck is good condition with stern broken away at the back, at the end of the number 4 hold. The bow lies northwest. The bell was recovered in 1992.

NYASALAND

GPS	50 23.53N 02 53.74W
TYPE	Steamship (Norwegian)
TONNAGE	383
CARGO	Coal
LENGTH	148ft
BEAM	26ft
DRAUGHT	9ft
DATE SUNK	1918.08.04
SEA DEPTH	55m

The ship was attacked by gunfire from U-boat 33 and sunk. The wreck has been positively identified by Lyme Bay Deep Divers. The stern is intact and lies to the north but the rest of the ship is broken up in the forward section of the vessel.

PERGO

GPS	50 16.65N 03 01.43W
TYPE	Motor vessel

TONNAGE	383
CARGO	Bagged fertilizer
LENGTH	157ft
BEAM	26ft
DRAUGHT	10ft
DATE SUNK	1975.01.02
SEA DEPTH	61m

The Pergo was in collision with the MV Zanzibar. The wreck lies upright and is intact. Identified by Lyme Bay Deep Divers. The bell was recovered in the net of a fishing boat.

PERRITON

GPS	50 24.18N 03 01.41W
TYPE	Sailing
TONNAGE	90
LENGTH	74ft
BEAM	21ft
DRAUGHT	10ft
DATE SUNK	1918.29.01
SEA DEPTH	48m

The Perriton was sunk by U-boat gunfire. She has a steam engine and large iron propeller. The wreck rises 8 metres at its highest point from the seabed.

PERRON

GPS	50 28.281N 03 22.852W
TYPE	Steamship (cable layer)
TONNAGE	3,342
CARGO	Ballast
LENGTH	290ft
BEAM	42ft
DRAUGHT	28ft

DATE SUNK	1917.01.09
SEA DEPTH	29m

The Perron was sunk by a torpedo and is very broken up. The stern section lies alongside the starboard side. The wreck lies on silt and visibility is not very good. The wreck rises 8 metres off the seabed. The bell has not been found and the wreck is very dispersed.

POMELLA

GPS	50 17.86N 03 00.99W
TYPE	Tanker
TONNAGE	6,766
CARGO	Crude oil
LENGTH	457ft
BEAM	57ft
DRAUGHT	31ft
DATE SUNK	1942.09.07
SEA DEPTH	59m

The vessel was part of convoy WP183, which suffered disastrous losses when attacked by German E-Boats operating from Cherbourg. The Pomella had an almost square shaped hull and the wreck lies on her starboard side with the deck in the vertical position and the bow to the west. There is a deep scour below the hull. (See also Buesten).

POMERANIAN (ex Grecian Monarch)

GPS	50 33.58N 02 41.43W
TYPE	Liner
TONNAGE	4,241
CARGO	Whiting and Fullers Earth.
LENGTH	381ft
BEAM	44ft
DRAUGHT	33ft
DATE SUNK	1918.15.04
SEA DEPTH	37m

Torpedoed en route London to Canada by the German submarine U-77 with the loss of 55. The wreck has been extensively salvaged. Located about 9 miles off Portland Bill

RADAAS (Harold's Wreck)

GPS	50 34.25N 03 04.91W
TYPE	Steamship (Danish)
TONNAGE	2,524
CARGO	Coal
LENGTH	290ft
BEAM	40ft
DRAUGHT	20ft
DATE SUNK	1917.21.09
SEA DEPTH	30m

The Radaas was torpedoed while on passage between Newcastle and Bordeaux. The wreck has deteriorated and collapsed but is a haven for marine life. The identity of the wreck has not been confirmed and could be the wreck of the Galia.

RECOIL

GPS	50 26.37N 02 44.02W
TYPE	Trawler (German)
TONNAGE	344
DATE SUNK	1940.28.09
SEA DEPTH	52m

The Recoil was a requisitioned (1940) German trawler. The vessel was used as an anti-submarine vessel and hit a mine while on patrol in Lyme Bay. The bow is SSE and the wreck is in two parts and contains numerous depth charges.

REGGESTROOM

GPS	50 21.56N 02 57.56W
TYPE	Steamship (Dutch)

TONNAGE	2,836
CARGO	Produce
LENGTH	101m
BEAM	14.69m
DRAUGHT	6.10m
DATE SUNK	1942.09.07
SEA DEPTH	53m

The Reggestroom was sunk after an attack by German E-Boats. The identity of the wreck is not confirmed and the vessel lies upside down.

ROMSDALEN

GPS	50 18.30N 02 44.42W
TYPE	Cargo ship (armed)
TONNAGE	2,548
CARGO	Coal, patent fuel blocks 3,500 tons
LENGTH	300ft
BEAM	40ft
DRAUGHT	18ft
DATE SUNK	1917.17.02
SEA DEPTH	57m

The ship was torpedoed. The wreck is a large freighter and lies upright with thousands of coal dust fuel blocks still in the hold. The identity has been confirmed by Lyme Bay Deep Divers.

ROSTEN

GPS	50 21.71N 02 58.06W
TYPE	Collier
TONNAGE	736
LENGTH	188ft
BEAM	30ft
DRAUGHT	12.7ft

DATE SUNK   1942.09.07

SEA DEPTH   55m

The wreck lies on port side and is twisted and collapsed. The collier has not been positively identified. The vessel was part of convoy WP 183. Also lost in the attack, were the Bokn, the Reggestroom, HMT Manor, the Pomella, the Gripfast and the Konshaug.

ROTA (local name the Bill Pitman)

GPS	50 24.98N 03 18.92W
TYPE	Steamship
TONNAGE	2,171
CARGO	Iron ore 3,600 tons
LENGTH	310ft
BEAM	45ft
DRAUGHT	18ft
DATE SUNK	1917,22.07
SEA DEPTH	50m

The Rota was torpedoed by the German submarine U-40. The ship's bell has been recovered. The wreck lists 20 degrees to the port side. There is extensive damage between the bow and the bridge.

ROTORUA 1

GPS	50 18.47N 02 59.73W
TYPE	Liner
TONNAGE	11,130
CARGO	General
LENGTH	484ft
BEAM	62ft
DATE SUNK	1917.22.03
SEA DEPTH	55m

The Rotorua 1 was torpedoed while on passage from New Zealand to London and is one of the biggest wrecks in the bay. She lies upright but has collapsed in many places, especially around the engine room. The top of the engine is the highest point of the wreck at 49 meters.

ROYAL ADELAIDE

GPS	50 34.67N 02 28.59W
TYPE	Sailing
TONNAGE	1,320
LENGTH	233ft
BEAM	38ft
DRAUGHT	23ft
DATE SUNK	1872. 25.11
SEA DEPTH	12m

The ship ran aground while on passage from London to Sydney (Australia). The wreck lies off the Chesil Beach and is very broken up. This early iron sailing vessel was driven onto the Chesil Beach during a severe southwest gale, on November 14 1872. Only five of the crew and passengers perished. The wreck lies about 100 yards off shore. (see Portland Map)

The Royal Adelaide was an immigrant ship bound for Sidney Australia. The weather was bad as she rounded Portland Bill on the night of the 24th November; the wind strong with bad visibility. The captain decided to seek the shelter of Portland. Due to the conditions, the Captain incorrectly interpreted his position and soon found himself off the Chesil Beach and not off Lulworth Cove as he had expected. The local coastguard lit flares from the beach to warn the Captain of the danger. The anchors were lowered to try and ride out the storm, but to no avail as they dragged in the severe conditions. Soon the ship ran aground, the pounding waves smashing the bottom of the ship onto the stone beach. The Adelaide rolled broadside onto the shore. The first mate bravely took a line in an attempt to swim to the shore but was soon overwhelmed by the storm seas and lost. The coastguard were able to put a line onto the ship with their rocket equipment, but the passengers, afraid of the sea would not trust the line. The Captain went first with a small child and reached the shore and, the apparatus rescued sixty before the line snapped. Slowly the ship broke up and those left on board were swept away by the sea. In total only seven of the passengers and crew were drowned, the casualties would have been much worse if it had not been for the mortar apparatus of the Portland Coastguard.

A major benefit of the wreck was the cargo of soap, coffee, sugar, cloth, brandy, gin and rum, which was soon washed onto the beach and eagerly gathered up.

SALSETTE

GPS	50 29.68N 02 43.09W
TYPE	Liner
TONNAGE	5,842
CARGO	General
LENGTH	440ft
BEAM	53ft
DRAUGHT	20ft
DATE SUNK	1917.20.07
SEA DEPTH	43m

The liner Salsette held the 'Blue Ribbon' for the fastest crossing of the Atlantic and was owned by the P&O Shipping Company. The ship was torpedoed while on passage for Bombay from London. There is a gun mounted on the stern, and plenty of portholes still remain on the wreck. It is slowly deteriorating and the internal structure of the ship is starting to collapse. The masts have fallen alongside the wreck and the ship is in two parts. This is a popular and recommended dive.

SARATOGA

GPS	50 36.02N 02 21.20W
TYPE	Trawler
SEA DEPTH	70ft
DATE SUNK	1981
SEA DEPTH	23m

The fishing vessel Saratoga sunk while under tow, only 4 miles from Weymouth harbour.

SAXMUNDHAM

GPS	50 21.86N 02.03.06W
TYPE	Steamship
TONNAGE	2537
CARGO	Coal and patent fuel blocks.
LENGTH	91.44m

BEAM	11.88m
DRAUGHT	7.77m
DATE SUNK	1888.11.04
SEA DEPTH	52m

Sunk after collision with Norwegian barque, Nor. Ten passengers and crew were drowned. The wreck lies upright but the deck has collapsed into the hull. The wreck has not been positively identified. The ship lies upright with a cargo of railway rolling stock. She has 47ft beam and two boilers (see Fluent.)

SCALDIS

GPS	50 34.28N 02 38.44W
TYPE	Trawler
LENGTH	80ft
DATE SUNK	1974.27.01
SEA DEPTH	35m

The trawler lies on her port side. She sank during heavy weather with all hands. The hatches of the wreck were pushed open by the sea, which caused the vessel to founder.

SEA VIXEN (Jet)

GPS	50 34.74N 02 26.96W
TYPE	Naval jet
SEA DEPTH	9m

This old naval jet was sunk for use in training exercises. The wings were taken off but the fuselage is intact. The bottom is very silty and easily disturbed.

SEVILLA

GPS	50 24.32N 03 22.93W
TYPE	Freighter (Spanish)
TONNAGE	1,318
CARGO	Wine and fruit (silver?)
LENGTH	260ft

BEAM	37ft
DRAUGHT	16ft
DATE SUNK	1918.24.04
SEA DEPTH	44m

The vessel is known locally as the Orange Man. The wreck lists to the port side at an angle of 20 degrees. The wreck is in good condition although it has been commercially salvaged. There are rumours that there is some silver among the cargo.

SIREN

GPS	50 12.44N 02 56.66W
TYPE	Sailing (iron)
TONNAGE	1,555
CARGO	General, barrels of China clay
LENGTH	75.59m
BEAM	11.58m
DRAUGHT	7.01m
DATE SUNK	1896.11.07
SEA DEPTH	60m

The wreck was identified by the recovery of the bell, in 1998. She sank after collision with HMS Landrail.

SPHENE

GPS	50 06.897N 01 38.730W
TYPE	Steamship coaster
TONNAGE	740
CARGO	Ballast
LENGTH	194ft
BEAM	30ft
DRAUGHT	11ft
DATE SUNK	1916.03.08
SEA DEPTH	68m

The Sphene was attacked by the German submarine U-18 under the command of Ober Leutnant Nelmeyer. He ordered the placing of scuttle charges, which sank the ship. The wreck has been positively identified.

ST DUNSTAN

GPS	50 38.27N 02 42.07W
TYPE	Dredger (Bucket)
LENGTH	200ft
DATE SUNK	1917.23.09
SEA DEPTH	27m

Commissioned as mine sweeper and sunk by mine. The vessel lies upside down and is broken up.

STANCREST (ex Shelldrake, ex Glenmor?)

GPS	50 26.80N 02 32.50W
TYPE	Freighter (aft engines)
TONNAGE	462
CARGO	Cement
DATE SUNK	1937.28.02
SEA DEPTH	46m

The cause of sinking is not known. The Stancrest sank while on passage from London to Bridgwater. Kingston BSAC and Lyme Bay Deep Divers have positively identified the wreck. The bell has been recovered but bears the initial of a previous owner. The wreck lies on her side and is very broken up.

START

GPS	50 28.28N 01 49.59W
TYPE	Coaster (Norwegian)
TONNAGE	728
CARGO	Coal
LENGTH	204ft
BEAM	29ft
DRAUGHT	11ft

DATE SUNK	1917.22.12
SEA DEPTH	40m

The Start was torpedoed. The wreck is very broken up is now very broken up and dispersed over a wide area. The stern lies on the port side.

STRYN (see Meat Boat)

SUDON

GPS	50 30.97N 02 25.60W
TYPE	Steamship (Swedish)
SEA DEPTH	14m

The Sudon has been extensively salvaged and broken up. The debris lies on a rocky seabed. There are no further details known of this wreck other than the name Sudon that was on the ship's bell.

THAMES

GPS	50 33.15N 02 27.15W
TYPE	Steamship
TONNAGE	408
CARGO	Crushed stone and ingots of tin
LENGTH	48.44m
BEAM	7.77m
DRAUGHT	4.11m
DATE SUNK	1891.02.01
SEA DEPTH	10m

The steamship struck the rocks and sank. There is not much left except plates and broken wreckage. Visibility is normally good.

TREVEAL

GPS	50 35.15N 02 04.90W
TYPE	Steamship
TONNAGE	5,243
CARGO	Manganese ore and jute

LENGTH	400ft
BEAM	15.95m
DRAUGHT	8.69m
DATE SUNK	1920.10.01

The Treval was en route from Calcutta to Dundee. She hit Kimmeridge ledges and stuck fast. The weather deteriorated and 22 crew drowned when a lifeboat capsized. The ship lost a total of 36 crew. The ship was later salvaged and is now very broken up.

The Treveal was on route from Calcutta to Dundee with a cargo of jute and ore. She came up the Channel with out a pilot, and in bad visibility made an error in her position, so laying a course, which eventually led her onto the ledges of Kimmeridge. The Treveal struck the ledges on 9th of January 1920. There was no panic and Little damage had been done. The Captain sent a signal for a tug to come and tow them off. By morning no tug had arrived and the weather had started to deteriorate. The waves were pounding into the side of the ship and there was a great danger of the vessel breaking up. The Captain gave the order to abandon ship, though did not realize that the Weymouth lifeboat was en route. In swell and storm the ships lifeboat capsized and 36 passengers and crew were drowned. The coastguard was found to have been negligent in their duty and one member was disciplined and dismissed from the service

TRITO

GPS	50 22.41N 02 44.20W
TYPE	Steamship
TONNAGE	1,057
CARGO	Coal
LENGTH	231ft
BEAM	36ft
DRAUGHT	13ft
DATE SUNK	1940.20.09
SEA DEPTH	58m

The Trito was built in 1921 with a triple expansion steam engine. She was bombed which killed 23 of the crew. The bows are blown apart and the wreck stands up to 10 metres above the seabed.

UB 772

GPS	50 24.70N 02 26.00W
TYPE	Submarine (German)
TONNAGE	761
LENGTH	67.06m
BEAM	6.10m
DRAUGHT	4.88m
DATE SUNK	1944.30.12
SEA DEPTH	51m

The submarine has not been positively identified. The sub is a late V11 C class vessel. The wreck is intact with a list to the port side. The submarine was attacked and sunk by allied bombers while on the surface.

UB74

GPS	50 31.82N 02 33.34W
TYPE	Submarine
TONNAGE	508
LENGTH	182ft
BEAM	19ft
DATE SUNK	1918.26.05
SEA DEPTH	34m

German submarine was attacked and sunk by depth charges from the armed yacht HMS Lorna. There has been extensive salvage off this wreck.

ULL (ex Ole Lea)

GPS	50 28.00N 02 45.24W
TYPE	Steamship (Norwegian)
TONNAGE	543
CARGO	Coal
LENGTH	168ft
BEAM	24ft
DRAUGHT	14ft

DATE SUNK	1917.04.07
SEA DEPTH	46m

The Ull was torpedoed while on passage from Glasgow to Nantes in France. The wreck is very broken up. The vessel was identified by Lyme Bay Deep Divers based on historic details with regards the engine.

UNKNOWN

GPS	50 38.08N 02 02.92W
LENGTH	30m
SEA DEPTH	28m

Known locally as the Landing Craft but it is definitely not this type of vessel. There is flush deck with six hatches, two petrol engines and a square bow with two towing eyes. The identity of this vessel is still a mystery. Any comments would be most welcome.

URSA

GPS	50 28.18N 03 00.57W
TYPE	Steamship (Swedish)
TONNAGE	1,740
CARGO	Coal
LENGTH	270ft
BEAM	37ft
DRAUGHT	19ft
DATE SUNK	1918.17.09
SEA DEPTH	46m

The identity of the wreck has been confirmed by Lyme Bay Deep Divers. The Ursa was torpedoed while en route from Penarth (South Wales) to Rouen (France). The bows are smashed, and the galley of the vessel can be seen towards the stern on the starboard side. The wreck has been mistaken as that of the WH Dwyer. The stern lies to the north.

US LANDING CRAFT

GPS	See Portland Map
TYPE	Landing craft

DATE SUNK	1944.13.10
SEA DEPTH	12m

You can dive this American Landing craft at slack water, 2 hours after Portland high water. The vessel lies 90 metres from the shore. The landing craft sank in a gale after engine failure, and nine of the crew drowned. The wreck hosts a variety of marine life. Entry and extraction from the sea can be difficult if the sea is not calm and waves are breaking.

VALDES

GPS	50 23.70N 02 24.46W
TYPE	Steamship
TONNAGE	2233
CARGO	Flour, Cattle and Fodder.
LENGTH	265ft
BEAM	40ft
DRAUGHT	17ft
DATE SUNK	1917.17.02
SEA DEPTH	50m

The Valdes was torpedoed and sank by the German submarine U-84. The wreck is 7 miles off Portland Bill. The steamer sank with the loss of six crew. The vessel has broken up into large sections.

VALENTINE TANKS

GPS	50 40.48N 01 54.64W
TYPE	Waterproof tanks

DATE SUNK   1944.04.04

SEA DEPTH   9m

Seven tanks sank while practising for the D-Day Landing during choppy weather. The tanks were fitted with a canvas collar, which sometimes leaked or were engulfed by waves. The position of the tanks are: 50 39.40N 01 53.35W; 50 40.08N 01 55.00W; 50 39.74N 0154.22W and 01 39.49N 01 53.31W.

VENEZUELA

GPS   50 36.60 N 01 43.60W

TYPE   Steamship (Argentine)

TONNAGE   730

CARGO   Coal 592 tons

LENGTH   190ft

BEAM   10.39m

DRAUGHT   3.29m

DATE SUNK   1918.14.03

SEA DEPTH   27m

The steamship was attacked and sunk by the German submarine UB-59. The wreck rises just over 4 metres off the seabed.

VENI

GPS   50 27.30N 02 24.12W

TYPE   Steamship (Norwegian)

TONNAGE   654

CARGO   Coal

LENGTH   53.98m

BEAM   9.02m

DRAUGHT   4.27m

DATE SUNK   1917.10.05

SEA DEPTH   40m

The vessel was attacked and scuttled after a German submarine attack. The wreck has not been positively identified.

W.H.DWYER

GPS	50 21.068N 03 06.000W
TYPE	Steamship, Great Lakes steamer
TONNAGE	1,770
CARGO	Ballast
LENGTH	250ft
BEAM	43ft
DATE SUNK	1917.26.08
SEA DEPTH	55m

The ship was torpedoed on passage from Rouen to Newport (Wales). The ship has been identified by Lyme Bay Deep Divers. The name of the vessel is on the stern, which is intact and lies to the north. The bridge, forecastle and deck have collapsed into the hull.

The back of this book contains editorial from those divers and businesses who helped provide much of the information contained in these pages and corrected mistakes.

WEY CHIEFTAN II

skipper Grahame Knott

WEYMOUTH based

The Wey Chieftain is a Weymouth based boat with a 700 hp Offshore 125. This gives the boat a vast and safe operating area, which includes the Channel Islands and Northern France. The boat has a large amount of deck space and is very quick.

Grahame is one of the leading dive boat skippers based at Weymouth. He has a deep knowledge of the local inshore and offshore wrecks and regularly takes out diving expeditions. In recent years he has been responsible for identifying a number of new and exciting deep-water wrecks. He regularly takes out mixed gas and technical dive groups and will undertake diving expeditions. Wrecks that he will visit include the MV Muree, an intact 1980 oil tanker, the Miniotta and HMS Amazon discovered last year. For visiting groups, Grahame is able to provide accommodation at his new divers' hostel which has recently opened.

Contact. Telephone 0103-771371/ 0966-242460

Email: grahame@weymouthoffshore.demon.co.uk

MISS PATTIE

Skipper John Walker

LYME REGIS based

John Walker is both a trawler man and dive skipper. He has a keen interest in the local shipwrecks and led the underwater excavation of the wreck of the Heroine, where a number of items were recovered, some of which are on display in the local museum. He can provide air and Nitrox, and recommend accommodation for diving groups. Regularly takes out divers all through the year. An ideally based boat for visiting the wreck of the Baygitano. John also has a local knowledge of the seabed and best reefs to visit.

Contact. Telephone.01297 552160/ 0797 0067236

SOUTHWEST DIVERS

Jeff King

EXMOUTH (East Devon)

The dive shop is located on the pier at Exmouth. They have their own RIB, and run diving trips throughout the year. The shop is well equipped with all dive requirements. They also run their own dive club and organise trips. They now have a second shop in Exeter. They regularly dive the Bretagne, Boma, Empress of India, the Lord Stewart and many other wrecks shown in the East Devon area. They also run dive courses.

Contact. Telephone 01395 268090

Email staff@southwestdivers.com

SWANAGE DIVER

Peter Williams

SWANAGE (East Dorset)

Swanage Diver is a 40' RIB. Peter is a locally based skipper operating from Swanage. He can offer some stunning scenic dives; his most popular dive site is the Kyarra.

Contact. Telephone 07977 142661/ 01929 423551

LINDY LOU

Ian Cornwall

WEST BAY (West Dorset)

Lindy Lou is a West Bay moored boat. The boat is run by Ian Cornwall, who can also provide air for visiting divers. A keen diver, Ian runs trips out to the local reefs and wrecks off West Dorset. His own favourite wreck is the Salsette and his recommended scenic area is " Saw Tooth Ledges".

Contact. Telephone 01308 423706

PORTLAND OCEANEERING.

The Old Waterside Bakehouse.

Castletown. Portland. Dorset. DT5 1BB

An old, established Portland dive shop. Ben Thomas is a local diver and Coastguard. The shop caters for all diving needs with air and mixed gas fills. Equipment repairs and testing can be done and they have a large stock of spares. The shop has an interesting display of locally found underwater artefacts and good selection of publications. The shop is centred in the area of Portland's main diving activity.

Contact. Telephone 01305-860402

Email. dive@portlando.demon.co.uk

ATLANTIS 2

Nick Bright

PAINGTON

Nick Bright is an East Devon based fisherman who with the help of local diver Simon Basset provided me with a number of corrections to the identity of some of the wrecks, such as the "Meat Boat". Nick takes out divers throughout the year on his boat Atlantis 2, an Offshore Pro 105. He will undertake charters, and is available for trips to all wrecks in the area of Lyme Bay and South Devon coast

Contact. Telephone 01803-524818/07899-916396

Email. nick@atlantis2.co.uk

Web site. *www.atlantis2.co.uk*

BLUE TURTLE

Douglas Lanfear

LYME REGIS

Doug is a keen diver/skipper who runs an Offshore Pro 105 out of Lyme Regis. He will take all categories of divers and is always interested in new wrecks. He can provide air and Nitrox, and will recommend accommodation.

Contact. Telephone 01297 34892

Email: doug@blueturtle.uk.com

Web site. *www.blueturtle.uk.com*

LYME BAY DEEP DIVERS

Lyme Bay Deep Divers are a group of wreck hunting enthusiasts who regularly organise deep-water wreck expeditions. In recent years this group have made some major finds, and have corrected and amended the identification of some of the wrecks off this coast. An exchange of information is always welcome and experienced divers can contact the group about forthcoming dives.

Contact. Tel 01823-288872

SHIPWRECK COVER ART WORK   By kind permission of Steve Martin

The front cover of this book is by Steve Martin, who is a marine architect based in Falmouth. He produces a number of maps of shipwrecks that have occurred off the English and Welsh coasts, and frameable prints and plans of a number of old wooden vessels. For a full list of the maps please go to the web site at.

www.njcpublications.demon.co.uk

The paddle steamer Bournemouth broken
on rocks at Portland Bill in 1886.